EX LIBRIS

The
ASTROLOGICAL
BIRTHDAY BOOK

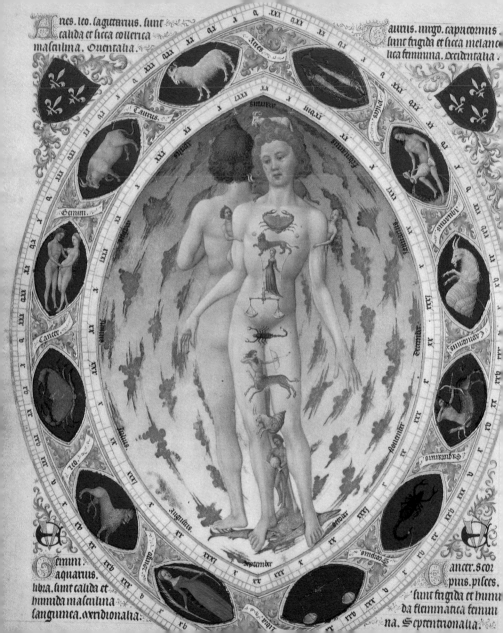

The

ASTROLOGICAL BIRTHDAY BOOK

A Permanent Diary of Treasured Dates

BY RHODA URMAN

HARRY N. ABRAMS, INC., PUBLISHERS
NEW YORK

Note: The dates applicable to each sign vary slightly from year
to year; the dates we have chosen for each sign are therefore
approximate

Frontispiece: An image of zodiacal man from a medieval Book
of Hours shows an androgynous central figure framed by the
zodiac, each part of the body marked with its ruling sign

Project Director: Hugh L. Levin
Editor: Margaret Donovan
Photo Editor: Eric Himmel
Designer: Ulrich Ruchti

Library of Congress Cataloging in Publication Data

Urman, Rhoda.
  Astrological birthday book.

   1. Zodiac.   2. Zodiac in art.   I. Title.
  BF1726.U75   133.5'2   81-14923
  ISBN 0-8109-0674-0   AACR2

Illustrations © 1982 Harry N. Abrams, Inc.

Printed and bound in Japan

CONTENTS

INTRODUCTION

Born in the region of the river Euphrates over 5,000 years ago, astrology evolved from the observations of celestial movement made by civilizations dependent upon natural rhythms for their very survival. It emerged from the star worship of the Akkadians and Sumerians, whose first astronomical observations were developed by the Babylonians into an astrological system of five planets. The Chaldeans perfected the system and became esteemed throughout the ancient world as astrologer-priests. With the fall of Babylonia, the Chaldean astrologers relocated their schools, and the science of astrology spread to Egypt, Greece, and Rome as well as to the Orient. The structure of astrology as we know it today was fixed by the Romans at the beginning of the Christian era. As new planets were discovered, astrological theory expanded to include a more sophisticated spectrum of experience appropriate to the modern age.

The early students of astrology used the knowledge derived from their observations of stellar and planetary movements to aid daily tasks like the determination of appropriate timing for planting and harvesting. Their repeated observations ultimately provoked a philosophical quest for a sense of order in the universe. If the seasons changed in a consistent pattern and the night sky exhibited constellations which could be identified and charted, then there must be some higher plan of which man could securely feel a part. Seeking to develop mastery over their fates, the pioneer astrological practitioners laid the foundation for a world view which slowly emerged, through centuries of

The astronomer from the *Psalter of Blanche of Castille* holds an astrolabe, crucial to calculations in astronomy

Cy comence Le c. xx i. chappitre
du huitiesme liure le quel parle
routes les planetes ot
double mouuement
dont lun leur est na
turel et propre qui

du double mouuement des p[l]
nettes et chascune en general
ment naturel ou quel elles sesso[r]
daler contre le firmamient. A[u]u[c]
des planetes parfont leurs cour[s]

amplification, into a vivid symbolism providing meaningful information about human experience.

The earliest artists employing astrological themes depicted the constellations in the already familiar animal and mythical forms selected by the first sky observers. Some of the most ancient renderings are on Babylonian boundary stones, or kudurru, circa 1100 B.C., which have recognizable symbols for Sagittarius, Capricorn, and Scorpio carved upon them. The Egyptians also systematized their astronomical observations into hieroglyphic forms utilizing familiar animals: the crocodile, hippopotamus, and jackal, for example. In turn, each culture from the Near to the Far East then fixed its own version of the zodiac into images either borrowed from the others or adapted to its own particular location.

It is from the Greek that we have the word "zodiac," meaning "little animal," and from Greek mythology that Western astrology for the most part derives its iconography. The heroes of Mt. Olympus became astrological symbols during the burst of Greek artistic advancement in the fifth century B.C. Adapting the Babylonian system, the Greeks identified the constellations and planets with the divinities whose names they bore. Since the gods were the ultimate heavenly masters, the planets belonged to them and had no names of their own, while most of the constellations remained in animal form. Artists of the Roman Empire then elaborated the Greek system and brought the symbols still in use today into common knowledge through sculpture, mosaics, and reliefs scattered throughout the Empire. Meanwhile, the Persian and Arab worlds were developing their own astrological iconography, derived from the Babylonians who had formerly occupied

In this pre-Copernican French manuscript, the planets, the Sun, and the Moon travel golden pathways between the signs they rule their lands. Eventually, Islamic artisans adapted the visual imagery of the astrological system to their own particular ethos, as in a thirteenth-century manuscript which shows a turbaned, scimitar-bearing god in place of a classical Greek Olympian.

When Christianity began its rise, astrology still exerted too powerful an influence throughout the ancient world for the new and struggling religion to uproot it. As a result, the twelve Apostles became conveniently identified with the twelve zodiacal signs. Much of the art found in monasteries, churches, cathedrals, and abbeys reflects this acceptance of the planetary system into church doctrine. From the seventh to the twelfth century, astrological themes even appeared in Byzantine manuscripts and church ceilings. The Vatican itself is amply decorated with astrological themes, as are the cathedrals of Notre Dame, Amiens, and Rheims in France and St. Mark's in Venice.

The twelfth century marked a resurgence of prestige for astrology, which became valuable once again for its own doctrines. After the Crusades, much new astrological information and imagery filtered into Europe through Spain and Sicily, although many iconographic details were changed through Middle Eastern interpretations. Also, Christian morality and the visual influence of the Middle Ages dictated fully clothed astrological gods, their classical nudity hidden behind fur-trimmed cloaks or armor.

With the renewed admiration for astrology and its support by princes and kings, astrological art flowered and assumed several significant forms. One was the microcosm, with man at the center of influences radiating from the planets and constellations circling around him and with each part of the body labeled according to the planet that controlled it. Such illustrations became prominent

The Sun surrounded by the Moon and the five visible planets decorates a late 12th-early 13th-century Iranian bowl of Minai'i ware

in the fourteenth century in calendars and then in prayer books like the *Très Riches Heures* of the Duc de Berry. Also common in Europe in the thirteenth and fourteenth centuries were astrological amulets and popular encyclopedias and texts on the medical uses of astrology.

The Renaissance brought vigor to the art of astrology as to all other artistic forms. The fervent use of celestial data to mark events is well illustrated by the fact that Pope Julius II actually based his coronation date on astrological indications. Astrology was venerated in artistic renderings throughout public buildings, churches, and princely mansions. Perhaps the most ambitious, if not the most dramatic, artistic interpretation of astrological data is the Agostino Chigi ceiling in Rome. This remarkable work reproduces Chigi's birth horoscope of December 1, 1466, and brings alive once again the recognizable deities of classical Olympus who embodied the planetary energies.

The widespread use of astrological themes in art culminated with the Renaissance and tapered off after the seventeenth century, when the "divine science" fell from grace once again. A later attempt at its revival was made in 1787 with the publication in London of Ebenezer Sibly's *A New and Complete Illustration of the Celestial Science of Astrology*. By and large, the Age of Enlightenment and empirical science succeeded in quashing the prestige that astrology had achieved during the Renaissance. While astrology was still discussed in farmer's almanacs and the like, graphic representations were quite limited and, when they did occur, often took on the appearance of caricature and cartoon. Only in the twentieth century, as art has sought to transcend the boundaries of traditional representation, have a few modern art-

A jumbled zodiac, symbolizing time, stretches across a medieval French illumination of Petrarch's "Triumph of Time Over Fame"

ists once more been drawn to the ancient symbolism of the stars.

The empirical mind scoffs at the idea that the positions of the planets and constellations can possibly have anything to do with what occurs on earth. This derision is not new; even scientists like Tyco Brahe and Isaac Newton had to justify their study of astrology. Perhaps at some future date scientists will discover some sort of electromagnetic wave theory to explain how planetary movements do indeed affect earthly experience. In the meantime, we might consider Carl Jung's theory of synchronicity: two events can occur which are apparently related by content and meaning, yet a causal relationship between them cannot be identified by scientific method. For example, why does a woman's menstrual cycle coordinate with the lunar cycle of twenty-eight days? Why do sunspots and solar flares affect radio transmission on earth?

These simple examples of synchronistic phenomena point out the hubris of modern man in thinking that the natural order can be fully understood by science alone. While science has helped our technological progress, it has not done much for the soul. In fact, it has so speeded things up, while simultaneously eliminating comfortable archaic beliefs, that it has left man abandoned without a sense of purpose in life. Astrology, which places value on intuitive knowledge extrapolated from within its symbolic language, has stepped in to rekindle man's sense of connectedness with the universe. It seeks to integrate man's place within the whole and guide him to a realization of the best possible use of his natal proclivities.

Using the data derived from the positions of the sun, moon, and other planets from the vantage point of earth, the astrologer charts the exact celestial configurations for any moment in time in a specific location. An individual's exact moment of birth is therefore crucial since his or her chart captures in a symbolic way the universal principles functioning at that moment, principles which will then be reflected in the newborn life. The mathematical relationships occurring among the planets and their placement in the chart form the factual basis for the interpretation of the horoscope. The interpretation then draws upon the complex language of symbolism that has evolved since Babylonian times.

There is one major advance that has benefited astrological interpretation in its current rebirth, and that is the knowledge we have gained from psychology. Astrology, as it is seriously practiced today, has moved away from the prediction of events, to focus more on the kind of energy patterns, existing from birth, which speak of the inner world. Since any planetary combination may symbolize a wide range of possibilities — although all within the framework of a general principle — it is quite difficult to predict the exact manifestation of a particular pattern. But what can be examined in depth is the intrinsic nature of the pattern, how it is likely to affect the life for good or ill, and how it may be used in the most constructive way. If unrealistic expectations are not demanded of the astrological lexicon, it can yield up unparalleled insight into individual character and life cycles.

It is absolutely imperative to stress the complexity of a precise astrological chart. When approached seriously, astrology simply cannot be reduced to the sun-sign form so prevalent in the media. Sun-sign astrology deals with only one factor in a very complicated picture: the sign in which the sun was located on

the day of one's birth. Since there are so many other variables to be taken into account when interpreting a chart, it is no wonder that people often react to sun-sign descriptions by remarking that they do not seem relevant at all.

Thus, it is necessary to bear in mind that the discussions of the signs in this volume describe individuals who are *types* of the sign; that is, they have a concentration of planets in that sign or emphasis on a planet which rules that sign. And an individual can be a type quite different from the sun sign he or she is born under. Within one individual there is usually a melange of a few different types. In any case, the sign descriptions are necessarily generalized because they do not deal with the specific case of an individual chart. What they do try to capture is the essence of the energy symbolized by that type in the context of the entire system. The zodiacal signs follow a natural rhythm of point and counterpoint, with each sign reacting to the one before and the one after. In this way, they embody a mandala of universal archetypes, connected to the seasonal patterns in the temperate zones where astrology was born.

In the final analysis, it must be said that astrology is a quasiscience which is as good as the art of the interpreter. Through the intuitive dexterity of an experienced and dedicated astrologer, it is an incomparable tool to self-knowledge. It also encourages tolerance of others because it helps clarify the incredibly diverse personalities of mankind. The practice of astrology does not foster abdication of personal responsibility; rather, it helps further self-reliance as it reveals and confirms one's particular way of being within the universal scheme. With this knowledge, one can make choices about whether or not an existing energy, or

A fierce Sun rules this unearthly scene from a 19th-century Thai astrological manuscript on the aspects of the Sun

tendency — even if it is a difficult one — will be used constructively or negatively.

The earnest use of astrology contributes to man's acceptance of himself so that he may develop his natural potential and so that he may feel more in tune with his place in the cosmos. Astrology has persisted into modern times and, in fact, is experiencing another renaissance, for there is no other theory as rich and varied which incorporates universal principles so descriptive and revealing of human character and behavior. It thus has achieved a majestic purpose which validates its long existence on earth and assures a continuing evolution in the future.

This Austrian clock of 1545 records, in addition to other astrological data, the cupping days (those propitious for letting blood)

THE SIGNS

Bartolommeo Passarotti's *Astrologer* beckons the viewer
into the arcane world of Renaissance astrology

ARIES MARCH 21 – APRIL 20

Ɏ Considered the first sign in the astrological lexicon of twelve, Aries symbolizes the primal energies apparent during springtime. After months of inactivity, the ground in spring stirs once again with a burst of renewed life. The thrust of tender shoots through the thawed earth marks the kind of emphatic activity associated with the sign of Aries, beginning approximately with the vernal equinox on March 21 and extending to April 20.

Since Aries is the starting point of the sun's annual cycle through the zodiac, it symbolizes beginnings in general, corresponding to the period of adolescence in human life. It represents the initial grappling with the world that an adolescent engages in while searching for an identity separate from the family matrix. This particular period of human development is well known for its rebellious self-assertiveness, rashness, boundless physical energy, and spirited desire to conquer, exhibited in sports as well as romance — all qualities contained within the fiery sign Aries.

Winter's transformation into spring, as adolescence into adulthood, is an animated process of intense activity. The Aries nature is instinctively invested in action and is not particularly comfortable with pure reflection. Aries types are pioneers, courageously forging into new territory, full of ideas for projects with themselves at the helm. However, since Aries embodies the element of fire, one inspired activity may soon die down and burn out for lack of sustained interest and perseverance, while a new one takes its place.

This constant round of activity helps the Aries type define itself. As the spring's new life juts forth from subterranean sources, so the self-assertive nature of Aries evolves from the hidden, subconscious realm of Pisces that precedes it. Such mysterious antecedents create a sense of insecurity for the Aries nature; only through the repeated pursuit of new enterprises does Aries experience a sense of self. By this constant testing of the self, Aries makes an impression on the world with an enthusiasm and a will to overpower all obstacles.

The ram, the symbol of Aries, butts his dramatic horns against whatever threatens him. The ram's nature makes him separate from the herd: he alone bears the responsibility of being the first to recognize danger, of taking action for survival, of leading the rest to safety. If challenged, both the ram and the Aries passionately rise to the occasion and fight. The one thing that will encourage Aries types to remain with any undertaking is a strong challenge, for combativeness is fundamental to them.

Ares, the Greek god of war, was easily provoked to rage and ready to strike swiftly if necessary. Astrologically, the sign of Aries is ruled by the red planet Mars, the namesake of the Roman warrior god. When opposed, the Aries type is fierce in self-defense. Although argumentative and easily enraged over minor situations, the type will usually not retain anger for long. When the battle cry is heard, the Aries leaps to attention with gusto, with a basic, instinctive defiance. Sensing, within, the vulnerability of the young shoot that has just gained a foothold on life, the Aries is prepared to protect it at all costs. The sometimes belligerent Aries exterior belies the uncertainty hiding beneath the arrogant heroics of youth.

Being so caught up in action, this first sign of the zodiac faces the essential challenge of developing consciousness of the self, from which will follow awareness of others. Unlike its polar opposite, Libra, Aries is not particularly accommodating to others. The type does best in a professional leadership role; intimacy and emotional sensitivity can prove difficult. If the cycle of persistent activity can be temporarily stopped, the Aries may become aware of the consequences of all this movement and change. A pause for reflection offers the possibility of the best channeling of Aries's considerable creative energy.

The plants ruled by this sign share the natural feistiness inherent in a strong Aries type. Among these are biting and pungent plants like radishes, peppers, garlic, onions, and mustard, and prickly and spiny ones like nettles and thistles.

The glyph for the sign (♈), which resembles two eyebrows linked with an elongated nose, can be taken to indicate the part of the body ascribed to the Aries influence: the head. It is thus said that the Aries type may be prone to headaches or to head injuries. Perhaps it is more appropriate to interpret Aries's rulership over the head as a symbolic call for this type to develop greater mental awareness in order to regulate the more heedless passions of its nature.

ARIES

MARCH

24 WILHELM REICH
Austrian psychiatrist

WILLIAM MORRIS
English artist; reformer

25 BÉLA BARTÓK
Hungarian composer

ARETHA FRANKLIN
American popular singer

26 TENNESSEE WILLIAMS
American playwright

DIANA ROSS
American popular singer

27 EDWARD STEICHEN
American photographer

SARAH VAUGHAN
American popular singer

28 MAXIM GORKY
Russian author

FRA BARTOLOMMEO
Italian painter

29 PEARL BAILEY
American popular singer

WILLIAM WALTON
English composer

30 VINCENT VAN GOGH
Dutch painter

FRANCISCO JOSÉ DE GOYA
Spanish painter

ARIES

Aries hic existimatur esse qui fryxum et
hellen transtulisse dicitur. Per helles pontu
quem hesiodus et pherecides habuisse auream
pellem. Dequa alibi plura diximus. Sed helle
decidisse inhelle spontum et neptuno con
pressam poenam pe
nonnulli eo
donum dixerunt. Prae
terea phryxum inco
luni adaeetam paenisse arietem
iovi immolasse pellem in
templo fuisse arietis

effigiem ipsius
Anube inter sidera constitutam habere
tempore antiquo frumentum seritur ideo qd
inotostum seu erit quae fuge maxime fuit causa.
Demonestenes dit arietem sibimet ipsi.

Auream pellem detraxisse et phryxo
memorie causa dedisse ipsum ad sidera
paenisse incirculo aequinoctiali constituens
capud adversus habens conversum
Occidens aprimis pedibus et exoriens in
fratri angulum qd supra diximus conlo
caxum pedibus prope con iungens caput
pistrici. Habet autem incapite stellam
unam. incornibus tres. incervice duas. in
pede priore deprimis unam. interscapula
quattuor incauda eius unam. inventre tres
inlumbis unam. inpede posteri eius unam.
Omnino sunt stellas. x. et. vii. Nonnulli
dixerunt pcreatum inoppido oratomeno
qd est inboeta. alii cretea dicunt
na tum naconum thesatie
et cathamantia. cumis
alii cum pluribus aeoli
filiis natum fuisse.

A quib: hinc subter possis cognoscere fultum.
I ma caeli mediam paste terit utprius illae.
C heletu pectus qd cernitur orionis.
E t ppe conspicies paruum subpectore clarae.

MARCH / APRIL

31
RENÉ DESCARTES
French philosopher

FRANZ JOSEPH HAYDN
Austrian composer

1
OTTO VON BISMARCK
German statesman

SERGEI RACHMANINOFF
Russian composer

2
CASANOVA
Venetian adventurer

ÉMILE ZOLA
French author

3
WASHINGTON IRVING
American author; diplomat

MARLON BRANDO
American actor

4
MUDDY WATERS
American jazz musician

DOROTHEA DIX
American social reformer

5
BETTE DAVIS
American actress

BOOKER T. WASHINGTON
American educator

6
HARRY HOUDINI
American magician

RAPHAEL
Italian painter

ARIES The author of this erudite 11th-century manuscript describes
the Greek origins of the constellation Aries

APRIL

7

BILLIE HOLLIDAY
American jazz singer

WILLIAM WORDSWORTH
English poet

8

JACQUES BREL
Belgian singer; composer

SONJA HENIE
Norwegian ice skater

9

CHARLES BAUDELAIRE
French poet; critic

VICTOR VASARELY
French painter

10

JOSEPH PULITZER
American newspaper publisher

CLARE BOOTH LUCE
American playwright; diplomat

11

JOEL GREY
American actor

CHARLES EVANS HUGHES
American statesman; jurist

12

HENRY CLAY
American statesman

JOHANNA SPYRI
Swiss author

13

THOMAS JEFFERSON
American statesman

SAMUEL BECKETT
Irish playwright

ARIES

Norton's *Ordinall of Alchymy* advises that to change lead into gold,
one should work when the Sun is in Aries, Taurus, or Gemini

APRIL

14
ARNOLD TOYNBEE
English economist; reformer

ANNE SULLIVAN
American educator

15
LEONARDO DA VINCI
Italian painter; engineer

HENRY JAMES
American author; critic

16
CHARLES CHAPLIN
English actor

WILBUR WRIGHT
American airplane inventor

17
J. P. MORGAN
American financier

WILLIAM HOLDEN
American actor

18
LEOPOLD STOKOWSKI
American conductor

CLARENCE DARROW
American lawyer

19
JOHN TAYLOR ARMS
American printmaker

RICHARD HUGHES
English author

20
JOAN MIRÓ
Spanish painter

HAROLD LLOYD
American comedian

ARIES

Pesellino's Mars in fury wears fanciful armor but is indubitably
of flesh and blood — the muscular, virile god who rules Aries

TAURUS APRIL 21 – MAY 21

Following Aries's burst of activity is the more measured second sign of the zodiac, Taurus. Now that its inspired predecessor has set all of nature's energies off to a good start, Taurus is equipped to tend springtime's seeds slowly to maturity. May's rich green foliage comes during Taurus's reign, from approximately April 21 to May 21 of each year.

The sign of Taurus is intimately connected with the soil and its fruits and is, in fact, the first of the earth signs to appear in the zodiac. While the germination of sprouts occurs as a sudden spurt, the full development of the plant is a more deliberate process. This energy of completion is symbolized by the Taurus type, who methodically works toward a goal of productive results. Because Taurus partakes of the element earth, these results are quite tangibly concrete.

As the second astrological sign, the Taurus type has a personality still young, still subject to strong primitive urges and steeped in the rites of spring. It is quite a sensual sign, concerned with reproduction as well as production, and the Taurus has the organization, foresight, constancy, and loyalty required for the successful bearing of progeny. Thus involved in building a sound, secure foundation to protect the fruits of its labors, the Taurean is often associated with financial gain and business enterprise. The Taurus type is inclined to accrue enough assets to insure peace of mind through a solid bank account. Taurean determination, ability to continue persistently in one direction, and pragmatic orientation help realize that goal.

However, prudent Taurus types who cultivate their gardens may at times dig furrows too deeply and find themselves stuck. Perhaps more than any other zodiacal type, the Taurus is most resistant to change. The very fixity of purpose that enables enormous productivity also fosters a stubbornness and hard-headedness that can be closed off to new information. Sometimes all too much a creature of habit, the Taurus type requires time to digest the unfamiliar, in the same way trees slowly yield up their fruit.

The lushness of May cannot help but provoke a sense of the power that lies behind all its profusion; this power is well expressed in Taurus's symbol, the bull. The bull suggests a rich lineage of symbolism reaching far into ancient times. Ancient Egypt worshiped the Apis bull. Ancient Crete had Minos, a half-man, half-bull king, son of Europa who had been abducted by Zeus camouflaged as a bull. Several archaic ceremonies centered around the bull represented joyousness over the reemergence of nature's luxuriance. (May Day celebrations are a more recent example of this surrender to a reawakened sensuality.)

The Taurean character celebrates the gamut of physical pleasures: nothing pleases this sign more than good food artfully prepared, physical love sensually experienced, and appealing objects plentifully collected. The Taurus must therefore guard against acquisitiveness and overindulgence of all the appetites. Moreover, Taurus types must learn to stretch their imagination beyond the concrete world of physicality, for they often deny the validity of emotional and spiritual experiences.

Although represented by the image of the bull, the sign of Taurus is considered a feminine sign, with connections to fertility

goddesses of the past. The reproductive and creative force of Taurus combines feminine receptivity with the prowess of the bull. Similarly, the glyph for Taurus (♉) can be seen in two ways. First, it abstracts the image of the bull with rounded head and horns. But it also symbolizes the blending of force with fecundity: the circle of the glyph is the sun, the masculine symbol, with the crescent of the moon, the feminine symbol, resting upon it.

This feminine energy is also reflected in the rulership of the planet Venus over the sign. Venus, the Roman goddess, symbolized spring and its fruitfulness; her Greek antecedent, Aphrodite, represented these qualities as well as beauty and love in all its manifestations. As a result, the Taurus is often artistically creative, drawing upon an instinctive sense of beauty to produce many splendid objects. At the least, the type usually possesses some kind of developed aesthetic sensibility.

The sign of Taurus is said to rule deep green plants like spinach, and spring flowers like daisies. Vegetables like beets, which almost taste of the earth itself, are also Taurean plants. The Taurean areas of the body are the neck, throat, and shoulders. Venus's influence and Taurus's rulership of the throat often combine to endow the Taurus with a sweet and melodic voice. Yet if, like the stubborn bull, the Taurean becomes more and more entrenched in a position, the tension that develops is commonly felt in the region of the neck and over the shoulders. The Taurean type is thus challenged to cultivate flexibility and open-mindedness into its garden along with an awareness of the cosmic forces that make the garden grow.

Evidence of a 13th-century revival of astrology, this Taurus comes from Southern Italy, where Eastern lore entered the West

TAURUS

APRIL

24   ANTHONY TROLLOPE
English author

BARBRA STREISAND
American singer; actress

25   ELLA FITZGERALD
American jazz singer

OLIVER CROMWELL
English statesman

26   MARCUS AURELIUS
Roman emperor

JOHN JAMES AUDUBON
American ornithologist

27   ULYSSES S. GRANT
American general; President

SAMUEL F. B. MORSE
American inventor

28   YVES KLEIN
French painter

LIONEL BARRYMORE
American actor

29   DUKE ELLINGTON
American jazz musician

WILLIAM RANDOLPH HEARST
American publisher

30   JACQUES LOUIS DAVID
French painter

H. M. QUEEN JULIANA
Dutch monarch

TAURUS

MAY

1 JOSEPH HELLER
American author

BENJAMIN HENRY LATROBE
American architect

2 BENJAMIN SPOCK
American author; pediatrician

CATHERINE THE GREAT
Russian czarina

3 NICCOLÒ MACHIAVELLI
Italian author; statesman

GOLDA MEIR
Israeli prime minister

4 AUDREY HEPBURN
Belgian actress

HORACE MANN
American educator

5 SÖREN KIERKEGAARD
Danish philosopher

KARL MARX
German social philosopher

6 SIGMUND FREUD
Austrian psychoanalyst

RUDOLPH VALENTINO
American actor

7 PETER ILYICH TCHAIKOVSKY
Russian composer

GARY COOPER
American actor

TAURUS   Venus, the ruler of Taurus, appears in a 12th-century Chinese
astrological manuscript called *Secrets of the Nine Luminaries*

MAY

8
HARRY S. TRUMAN
American President

ALPHONSE LEGROS
French painter

9
JOSÉ ORTEGA Y GASSET
Spanish author; philosopher

ALBERT FINNEY
English actor

10
FRED ASTAIRE
American dancer

DAVID O. SELZNICK
American film producer

11
SALVADOR DALI
Spanish painter

MARTHA GRAHAM
American choreographer

12
FLORENCE NIGHTINGALE
English nurse

EDWARD LEAR
English humorist

13
JOE LOUIS
American boxer

DAPHNE DU MAURIER
English author

14
ROBERT OWEN
British social reformer

TIMOTHY DWIGHT
American clergyman

TAURUS   Each of 36 Eastern decans rules ten degrees of the zodiac: here, from
a Renaissance fresco, is Taurus with one of its decans

MAY

15
KATHERINE ANNE PORTER
American author

JASPER JOHNS
American painter

16
HENRY FONDA
American actor

JOHN SELL COTMAN
English painter

17
ERIK SATIE
French composer

JOHN PENN
American patriot

18
BERTRAND RUSSELL
English philosopher; reformer

MARGOT FONTEYN
English ballerina

19
NELLIE MELBA
Australian opera singer

FRANK CAPRA
American film director

20
HONORÉ DE BALZAC
French author

JOHN STUART MILL
English economist; philosopher

21
ALBRECHT DÜRER
German painter; engraver

FATS WALLER
American jazz musician

TAURUS   A French needlepoint hanging from the 1680s portrays a figure
of Spring, circled by Aries, Taurus, and Gemini

GEMINI MAY 22 – JUNE 21

Ⅱ The third sign of the zodiac, Gemini, proves the adage "Man does not live by bread alone." The preceding sign, Taurus, has carefully tended the wheat so that Gemini can now develop other faculties. The energy of Gemini is symbolically linked with the rational mind. The first sign appearing in the element of air, it is reflective of the mellow breezes of early summer when the air comes alive with a profusion of newly hatched insects. This is the time of year from approximately May 22 to June 21.

Not only is Gemini the first of the air signs, but it is also the first sign to be symbolized by human form, the Twins. (The only other two signs which share this human representation are Virgo and Aquarius.) Thus, Gemini offers the clearest example of the power that differentiates man from beast: the human intellect. It is this emerging cerebral activity that typifies the function of Gemini, who sorts through the myriad stimuli in the environment and starts to perceive relationships between them.

Since Gemini embodies the quickening of human intelligence, it is often compared to the image of a butterfly riding the wind from flower to flower, garnering what it may at each landing. And, indeed, the Gemini does ride the currents of the mind, quickly absorbing, cataloguing, and correlating all that it perceives. Intensely curious, the Gemini type is in need of constant mental stimulation. Boredom is anathema to Gemini; this type will energetically seek out contacts with many people and often be involved in more than one activity simultaneously.

Because the element of water has not yet been introduced into the zodiac, Gemini pursues its mental meanderings without an emotional investment. Hence, the mercurial mind of the Gemini type can be lacking in depth and constancy, which can create a kind of superficiality in personal relationships as well as in endeavors. As the curious butterfly seeks undiscovered nectar, so the blithe Gemini type may not remain with any one person or situation for long. Nervous exhaustion and feelings of detachment sometimes result from Gemini's unabated quest for mental stimulation.

Having surpassed the more instinctual natures of Aries and Taurus, Gemini utilizes the rational mind for scientific inquiry, identifying patterns and designs within a complex of information. The Gemini type does not accept things on faith, but needs to test ideas by empirical experience. By thus finding a framework for the vast variety of nature, the Gemini seeks to order the chaos of an excessive cerebral input. Often the first to sniff a change in the wind, the Gemini type frequently displays a talent for contemporary design and fashion. This air element can also contribute to musical ability or a talent for drawing, the immediate translation to paper of environmental impressions.

The symbol for Gemini, the Twins, signifies the dualistic nature of the sign. Gemini is facile at putting things together in a meaningful way because the type embodies the idea of twinship, of related yet separate elements coexisting side by side, of more than one energy functioning at a time. This suggests the ultimate challenge for the Gemini type: to achieve a unity of focus while drawing upon the scattered threads of many mental investigations. The Twins in the constellation of Gemini are the brothers Castor

and Pollux, who were honored throughout ancient Greece as the Dioscuri, the tutelary divinities of sailors and the guardians of hospitality. Astrologically, this origin links Gemini with sibling and neighborhood relationships and with education.

That Gemini is one of the signs associated with learning is further revealed in its rulership by the planet Mercury. Mercury was the Roman version of the Greek Hermes, winged messenger of Zeus and god of travelers and commerce. Through his connection with merchants and trade, Hermes polished the art of eloquent communication, and his duties have come to symbolize the Gemini type's dexterity with words. Avid in reading, writing, speaking, teaching, and learning languages, Gemini enjoys wit and playing with words which, like quicksilver, slip off the tongue and suddenly change form.

The glyph for Gemini (II) represents the twins and the Roman numeral two. Perhaps more relevantly, it can be abstracted to mean the door leading to Gemini's domain of conscious awareness. In nature, Gemini's interest in the interaction of separate but related entities causes it to rule connective growths like grass, weeds, and woodbine.

Gemini holds dominion over the hands, arms, lungs, and nervous system. The sign's profuse perceptions of connections between man and the environment enabled man to fashion tools with his hands and to thereby extend his field of experience. The hands and arms are capable of combining in countless permutations; Geminis, however, must learn to relax when mental circuits are overburdened. They must appreciate that, unlike the butterfly, they can be left gasping for breath from their ceaseless peregrinations.

In a detail from a late 19th-century Indonesian astrological calendar, the Gemini twins romp above a representation of Cancer

GEMINI

MAY

25
RALPH WALDO EMERSON
American author

BEVERLY SILLS
American opera singer

26
JOHN WAYNE
American actor

ALEXANDER PUSHKIN
Russian poet

27
ISADORA DUNCAN
American dancer

RACHEL CARSON
American author; biologist

28
IAN FLEMING
English author

DIONNE SISTERS
Canadian quintuplets

29
JOHN F. KENNEDY
American President

BEATRICE LILLIE
British comedienne

30
CORNELIA OTIS SKINNER
American actress; author

BENNY GOODMAN
American musician; bandleader

31
WALT WHITMAN
American poet

ELLSWORTH KELLY
American painter

GEMINI

JUNE

1
MARILYN MONROE
American actress

JOHN MASEFIELD
English poet

2
THOMAS HARDY
English author

EDWARD ELGAR
English composer

3
ALLEN GINSBURG
American poet

JOSEPHINE BAKER
American entertainer

4
ROBERT MERRILL
American opera singer

ROSALIND RUSSELL
American actress

5
ADAM SMITH
Scottish economist

JOHN MAYNARD KEYNES
English economist

6
THOMAS MANN
German author

PETER LORRE
Hungarian actor

7
AL JOLSON
American popular singer

BEAU BRUMMELL
English dandy and wit

GEMINI   In this Spanish fresco, Mercury rides across the sky in a chariot
bearing cameos of Gemini and Virgo, the planet's signs

JUNE

8   FRANK LLOYD WRIGHT
American architect

PAUL GAUGUIN
French painter

9   COLE PORTER
American composer

PIETER SAENREDAM
Dutch painter

10   JUDY GARLAND
American singer; actress

GUSTAVE COURBET
French painter

11   RICHARD STRAUSS
German composer

JACQUES COUSTEAU
French oceanographer

12   ANNE FRANK
German-Dutch diarist

CHARLES KINGSLEY
English author; clergyman

13   WILLIAM BUTLER YEATS
Irish poet; playwright

BASIL RATHBONE
English actor

14   HARRIET BEECHER STOWE
American author

MARGARET BOURKE-WHITE
American photographer

GEMINI   Victor Brauner was drawn to androgynous imagery from astrological and mythological sources, as in this *Gemini* (1938)

JUNE

15
SAUL STEINBERG
American painter

EDVARD GRIEG
Norwegian composer

16
STAN LAUREL
English comedian

JOYCE CAROL OATES
American author

17
IGOR STRAVINSKY
Russian-American composer

CHARLES GOUNOD
French composer

18
PAUL McCARTNEY
English singer; songwriter

ALLART VAN EVERDINGEN
Dutch painter

19
WALLIS WARFIELD SIMPSON
American, Duchess of Windsor

BLAISE PASCAL
French scientist; philosopher

20
LILLIAN HELLMAN
American playwright

JACQUES OFFENBACH
French composer

21
JEAN-PAUL SARTRE
French philosopher; author

ROCKWELL KENT
American illustrator

GEMINI

Antoine Watteau's allegory of summer portrays Ceres
surrounded by Leo, Cancer, and Gemini

CANCER JUNE 22 – JULY 23

The sign of Cancer falls amidst the ripening languor of summer, when the sun has reached its highest point over the northern hemisphere. The longest days, the lingering of the sun for a while at this point before turning back, hail the summer solstice which is the beginning of Cancer. The energy of Cancer, introducing the element of water into the zodiacal pattern, slows down the vivacious explorations of Gemini. This highly emotional sign predominates from approximately June 22 to July 23 each year.

The element of water brings with it the personal world of emotions, thus far dormant in Cancer's predecessors. Aries set forth the individual spark of action; Taurus strengthened this beginning with material productivity; Gemini then quickened the use of the mind. Now the growth of the self is further developed with the addition of feelings. The markedly sensitive Cancer type functions primarily on the level of emotions; for this type, feelings are as tangible and necessary as objects of the material world. In fact, a Cancer type whose emotional life is hindered may become a collector of objects to fill the interior void.

The world of the impressionable Cancer is inextricably linked with the home and mother, as the underwater security of the crab (its symbol) is dependent upon the "shell" it carries on its back. This is a sign representing the family matrix, ancestry, and the past. Cancer sets limits on the unrestricted wanderings of Gemini, much the same as a mother must set certain necessary limits on her child's adventures. It is a sign of protective nurturing, sheltering from external harm. Cancers usually have a strong sense of family ties, even if it is only an intense awareness of their own history and how that history remains an integral part of them forever.

Because of the Cancer type's yearning for security and self-protection, this is not a sign which readily accepts others into its ken. A Cancer type will be circumspect about most relationships. Only when someone is perceived as worthy of "joining the family," through the test of time, will a Cancer let down defenses. Strong bonds of love and duty are engendered within the family, of which the Cancer type can be caringly supportive, as long as those feelings are reciprocated. If not, the delicate balance in the watery depths will be upset and the Cancer may become prone to melancholy or psychosomatic discomforts.

The sign's association with the maternal function makes the quality of their childhood crucial to the future well-being of Cancers. Cold, punitive, or unreliable parenting is particularly damaging to them. Concerned with their own childhoods, Cancers are usually exceptionally involved in the lives of their children. They can be emotionally possessive, as the crab can tenaciously hold on with its claws. The challenge for this sign is to be able to love without holding the loved one captive through overprotectiveness and smothering.

Like Pisces, Cancer has its roots in the depths of the sea, the universal mother of life. Intangible impressions coalesce from the watery sensibility of this sign—as the first cell of life did from the primal seas eons ago—so that Cancer types may experience psychic perceptions. At the least, their sensations have the quality

of immediate presence, and those felt long ago can easily be brought to life as though just encountered. The retentiveness of the crab contributes to this adept memory.

According to legend, the crab was awarded its place in the heavens after aiding Hercules in battle by biting his enemy on the foot. Significantly, the immortal who so honored the crab was Zeus's wife, Hera, the Greek goddess of marriage and maternity. In the Roman pantheon, this goddess was Juno, similarly a goddess of childbirth. As the feminine principle of heavenly light, Juno was also a moon goddess, revealing the planetary rulership of the moon over Cancer.

The moon, embodying the feminine or yin principle, aptly symbolizes the maternal function of Cancer. The moon is a reflector, without light of its own and therefore dependent upon the solar center, as the Cancer type is upon its home. The moon's constant fluctuations in its monthly phases place it in a different zodiacal sign every few days. Its fast pace is reflected in the frequent changes of mood experienced by the Cancer type.

The glyph for the sign of Cancer (♋) symbolizes the folded claws of the crab, the union of sperm and egg, and the breasts, the part of the body Cancer rules. The food of human nurturing comes from the breasts and indicates the Cancer's special relationship to food, for this type can be prone to aberrant eating habits or stomach trouble.

In the plant world, Cancer holds sway over plants that grow in water, like water lilies, as well as cucumbers, squash, and melons. Similar to these plants full of water, the Cancer is full of emotions which, when fed within a nurturing relationship, flower in large, full blooms.

One born with the Moon and Venus in Cancer, according to this Arabic manuscript, will have pale skin, red cheeks, and a round face

CANCER

JUNE / JULY

CANCER

JULY

3   FRANZ KAFKA
German author

GEORGE SANDERS
English actor

4   LOUIS ARMSTRONG
American jazz musician

NATHANIEL HAWTHORNE
American author

5   JEAN COCTEAU
French author; director

WANDA LANDOWSKA
Polish-French pianist

6   NICHOLAS I
Russian emperor

JOHN PAUL JONES
American naval hero

7   RINGO STARR
English popular singer

VITTORIO DE SICA
Italian film director

8   JOHN D. ROCKEFELLER
American industrialist

JEAN DE LA FONTAINE
French fabulist

9   DOROTHY THOMPSON
American journalist

DAVID HOCKNEY
English painter

CANCER   In this pastoral scene from the Duchess of Burgundy's *Book of Hours*, peasants make hay by a river under the sign of Cancer

JULY

10
JOHN CALVIN
French theologian

MARCEL PROUST
French author

11
JOHN QUINCY ADAMS
American statesman

YUL BRYNNER
Russian-born actor

12
HENRY DAVID THOREAU
American author

JULIUS CAESAR
Roman statesman

13
KENNETH CLARK
English art historian

HAILE SELASSIE
Ethiopian emperor

14
INGMAR BERGMAN
Swedish film director

EMMELINE PANKHURST
British suffragette

15
REMBRANDT VAN RIJN
Dutch painter

IRIS MURDOCH
English author

16
MARY BAKER EDDY
American Christian Scientist

JEAN-BAPTISTE COROT
French painter

CANCER   Among portrayals of astrological motifs, this German plate illustrating Cancer is unusual for its comic quality

JULY

17
JOHN JACOB ASTOR
American merchant

JAMES CAGNEY
American actor

18
JOHN GLENN
American astronaut

WILLIAM M. THACKERAY
English author

19
MARC CHAGALL
Russian-born painter

EDGAR DEGAS
French painter

20
THEDA BARA
American actress

PETRARCH
Italian poet; humanist

21
ERNEST HEMINGWAY
American author

ISAAC STERN
American violinist

22
STEPHEN VINCENT BENÉT
American poet

ALEXANDER CALDER
American sculptor

23
RAYMOND CHANDLER
American author

PHILIPP OTTO RUNGE
German painter

CANCER   A Gothic stained-glass quatrefoil from Austria shows the Moon (Cancer's ruler), the Sun, and two stars

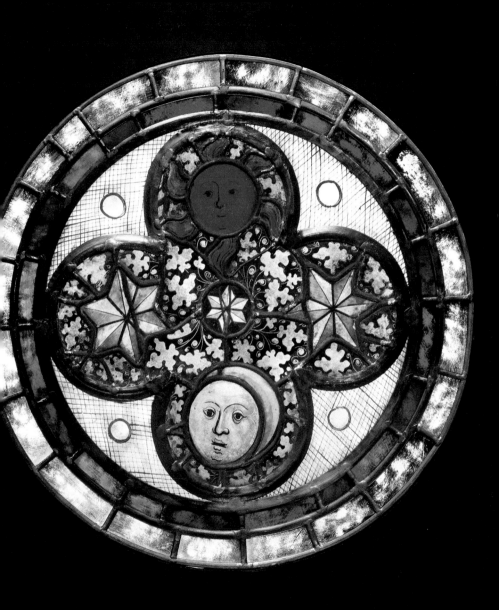

LEO JULY 24 – AUGUST 23

♌ The second of the fire signs appearing in the zodiac is Leo, bringing the heat of high summer with the most intense solar rays. Now that Cancer has rounded off the attributes of the fundamental personality, Leo is ready to expand human development through the process of individuation. The Leo type profits from the security established under Cancer's nurturing, and now bursts forth into the world ready to present itself and see how the world will react. The time of year bringing an indulgent and welcome pause before the fall harvest is Leo's, from approximately July 24 to August 23.

During this time of relaxation before autumn, the Leo personality has the opportunity to explore the best avenues for personal self-expression. As a result, this type often is involved in artistic pursuits which provide a vehicle for the Leo's unique vision to be brought into the world. The interaction with that external world is quite important to Leo, for the activities engaged in must receive acknowledgement and appreciation. Unlike the water signs, which might be content with a purely private creative process, the Leo type needs fond recognition to feel fulfilled.

One of the ways the Leo type tries to assure this applause is through a sense of the dramatic. Theatrically utilizing the legacy of fire, the Leo stages its feats with passionate intensity. This sign is thus often associated with the performing arts. The Leo ability to project an inspired radiance is a definite asset on the stage as well as in the political arena, for the king of beasts often becomes a leader of men.

Feeling a kinship with the sun itself, Leos assume their position at the helm has been awarded by divine right. On the one hand, this characteristic can enable Leos to encourage and support their followers to deeds of valor and nobility; on the other, it can make them autocratic and hard rulers who arrogantly refuse to give ear to any debate on issues they have already decided. This trait reveals the tendency to stubbornness Leo shares with Taurus, Scorpio, and Aquarius, related signs within the astrological system.

Astronomically, one of the prominent stars in the Leo constellation is Regulus, "the little king." The Leo's sense of natural kingship can give rise to visions of royal splendor. Eager to exhibit this pride of position, the Leo may dramatically sport flamboyant dress, luxurious golden accessories, or marks of distinction that will capture the necessary regard. If successful in this, the Leo type will beam back an affection and loyalty that makes this sign so endearing. If unnoticed, the haughty beast may slink away in a petulant snit.

Many early civilizations were drawn to the symbolism of the proud lion, and ancient lore is replete with this animal. As symbols of Roman power, lions were used to vanquish enemies of the state as well as the early Christians. To battle the formidable power of the Nemean lion was the first of Greek Hercules's twelve labors. In the Far East, the lion became the Oriental dragon. In ancient Egypt, the sun entered the sign of Leo at a time when the waters of the Nile rose and the lions would emerge from the parched deserts to refresh themselves by the cool riverbanks.

The lion's sultry habitat reveals the planetary ruler of Leo, for

it is the sun that holds sway over the yellow-maned king of the jungle. As the moon is the archetypal yin or feminine principle, so the sun is the archetypal yang or masculine principle. The sun is the center of our universe and provides a primal creative energy without which there would be no life. It represents the paternal energy, the will, power, and desire that are embodied in the act of creation and that seeks the maternal energy for completion. (As a result, children themselves are regarded by the Leo type as one form of creative self-expression.) Several ancient solar deities had characteristics analogous to those of Leo: the vigorous, courageous Babylonian god Shamash; the Egyptian Ra, creator and ruler of the world; the Roman Janus, father of all the gods. Their enormous creative potential and will to make it manifest are also seen in the Leo. This relationship to the solar deities clarifies the Leonine need to be the center of attention which, when recognized, inspires the ardent Leo to ever more noteworthy achievements.

The glyph for Leo (♌) represents the powerful tail of this special animal. While the glyph for Cancer has a feeling of enclosure, the one for Leo conveys a feeling of outflowing movement. This quality is also expressed by the part of the body ruled by the sign of Leo: the heart, the human "sun," the center from which flows the vital fluid of life. If this heart center is inadequately stimulated, the regal lion will deflate into a lowly beast faster than any other.

In nature, Leo reigns over bright golden plants such as camomile, daffodils, marigolds, and the vermilion poppy. It rules mistletoe as well, the plant used to engender some of the heat of August in the heart at Christmastime.

In an Indian miniature, a peri holding a golden solar disk sits upon a striding Leo composed of human and animal figures

LEO

JULY/AUGUST

27

PEGGY FLEMING
American ice skater

ALEXANDRE DUMAS, FILS
French author

28

BEATRIX POTTER
English author; illustrator

JACQUELINE KENNEDY ONASSIS
American First Lady

29

ALEXIS DE TOCQUEVILLE
French politician; author

DAG HAMMARSKJÖLD
Swedish statesman

30

EMILY BRONTË
English author

HENRY FORD
American industrialist

31

EVONNE GOOLAGONG
CAWLEY
Australian tennis player

MILTON FRIEDMAN
American economist

1

HERMAN MELVILLE
American author

FRANCIS SCOTT KEY
American poet

2

JAMES BALDWIN
American author

MYRNA LOY
American actress

LEO

AUGUST

3
RUPERT BROOKE
English poet

STANLEY BALDWIN
English statesman

4
PERCY BYSSHE SHELLEY
English poet

QUEEN MOTHER ELIZABETH
English royalty

5
GUY DE MAUPASSANT
French author

JOHN HUSTON
American film director

6
ALFRED LORD TENNYSON
English poet

LUCILLE BALL
American comedienne

7
MATA HARI
Dutch spy

NATHANAEL GREENE
American Revolutionary general

8
ANDY WARHOL
American painter

CHARLES BULFINCH
American architect

9
JOHN DRYDEN
English poet; playwright

JEAN PIAGET
Swiss psychologist

LEO
The calendar of the *Belles Heures* of the Duke of Berry is notable for its delicate gold tracery, which here ensnares a proud Leo

Juillet a xxxi. jours.
Et la lune xxix.

xix.	g		saint thibaut
viij.	A	iiij	saint proces
	b	iij	saint apolin.
xvj.	c	ij	saint martin.
v.	d	ix	saint dominique
	e	viij	Oct. saint pierre S. pol.
iiij.	f	Nõs	saint thomas.
ij.	g	id	saint claude
	A	id	saint zenon.
x.	b	id	les vij. freres.
	c	id	saint benoit.
xviij.	d	id	saint silt
vij.	e	id	saint wistin
	f	id	saint naalt.
xv.	g	jd	saint florenan.

AUGUST

10
HERBERT HOOVER
American President

NORMA SHEARER
American actress

11
HUGH Mac DIARMID
Scottish poet

CHARLOTTE M. YONGE
English author

12
CECIL B. DE MILLE
American film director

EDITH HAMILTON
American author

13
ANNIE OAKLEY
American theatrical performer

ALFRED HITCHCOCK
Anglo-American film director

14
JOHN GALSWORTHY
English author

CLAUDE VERNET
French painter

15
NAPOLEON BONAPARTE
French emperor

JULIA CHILD
American chef

16
T. E. LAWRENCE
English adventurer

AGOSTINO CARRACCI
Italian painter

LEO

Pegasus supports an astronomical globe of 1579;
visible here is the summer zodiac from Gemini to Leo

AUGUST

17	**MAE WEST** American actress **ROBERT DE NIRO** American actor
18	**ROBERT REDFORD** American actor **SHELLEY WINTERS** American actress
19	**ORVILLE WRIGHT** American airplane inventor **OGDEN NASH** American poet
20	**BENJAMIN HARRISON** American President **EERO SAARINEN** Finnish-American architect
21	**COUNT BASIE** American jazz pianist **H.R.H. PRINCESS MARGARET** English royalty
22	**CLAUDE DEBUSSY** French composer **DOROTHY PARKER** American author
23	**GENE KELLY** American dancer **LOUIS XVI** French monarch

LEO   The Sun card — this one from the famous Visconti Tarot deck (Cremona, 1484) — depicts the ruler of Leo

VIRGO

♍ After the glitter of Leo, a very different sort of energy emerges into the zodiacal pattern. Virgo's nature is in direct opposition to the pleasure-loving Leo's, for it comes at the beginning of the fall harvest when there is much crucial work to be done. In fact, the period from approximately August 24 to September 23 generally connotes the return to serious endeavor, work, and school, and that is Virgo's time.

Early fall brings an end to the self-glorification that marked Leo because the season of the harvest necessarily concerns the collective welfare. With a humble awareness of the responsibility for bringing the winter's food supply safely in from the fields, Virgo is equipped to serve dutifully and work hard. The second sign in the element earth, Virgo represents, like Taurus, a resourceful approach to the accomplishment of tasks. But it adds other factors: a more developed social awareness and a will to perfection.

Failure to achieve perfection leaves the Virgo naggingly dissatisfied. Unlike Leos, who are so dependent on others' applause, Virgo types are hardest on themselves when weighing the quality of their own performance. This inherent need for critical self-evaluation leads Virgos to attempt self-perfection, with the hope that their high standards will branch out into the world. If their hopes are not fulfilled, Virgo's critical faculties may be not only self-directed but may also be used unsparingly in judging others. The major difficulty with Virgo is that this type can be carping about imperfections and highly critical, focusing on minute flaws instead of recognizing the acceptability of the overall picture. Yet, one constructive expression of this exacting trait is the exceptional craftsmanship which Virgos often display in their work.

The sign was named from the Greek legend of Erigone. Erigone, daughter of Icarius, went with her dog in search of her father's tomb after he had been slain. When she finally discovered it, she hanged herself in despair. Dionysus saw to it that Erigone and her dog were carried to the heavens and fixed there as, respectively, the constellation Virgo and the star Procyon. Perhaps it is this legendary bond that makes Virgos so often fond of pets.

The sign of Virgo is the second sign to be symbolized in human form; its symbol is a maiden (Erigone) bearing a shaft of wheat or an ear of corn. Virgo's leanings toward purism stem from the maiden's state of perfect chastity. The symbol of the virgin appears throughout antiquity and into the modern world. Awareness of the latent potency contained within this sign is aptly symbolized by the Egyptian sphinx, with the body of a lion and the head of a maiden. This creature is said to represent the cusp, or changeover, from Leo to Virgo, holding the power of the lion in check with the demure mentality of the virgin. In Rome, the Vestal Virgins were honored priestesses who took severe vows of chastity under penalty of death. They spent ten years under instruction to perfect the performance of their duties, then later taught the neophytes themselves.

While there is currently some debate as to the planetary rulership for this sign, Virgo's desire for knowledge and interest in education are usually thought to stem from Mercury's traditional placement as its ruler. Mercury's rulership over Gemini is seen in that sign's swift and versatile intelligence; in Virgo, Mercury's

energy brings a more practical and precise mentality. Discriminating among many details in order to arrive at an analytical diagnosis is the facility of Virgo.

Hermes, the Greek antecedent of Mercury, carried the caduceus, a winged staff with two serpents wound around it. In ancient Babylonia the caduceus symbolized wisdom and the gift of healing. Apollo gave it to Hermes to celebrate their long friendship and especially Hermes's devoted helpfulness. The caduceus and Hermes's quality of solicitous concern have come to reflect Virgo characteristics, for these types are strongly drawn to performing some service in their work. The caduceus has now become the signature of the medical profession, and Virgo types are often found in medicine, nursing, nutrition, and the counseling professions. Virgo thus represents the acumen of Mercury placed at the service of others.

In the natural world, Virgo rules plants like wheat, millet, corn, oats, and rye — the basic grains of the harvest. These foods reflect the simplicity and purity of diet which Virgo types like to follow. The glyph for the sign (♍) symbolizes the serpentine sexual energy with the organ of maidenhood closed off to penetration. Synchronistically, the glyph echoes the "m" form which calls to mind the most revered of Virgins, Mary, mother of Jesus.

While it may not always be apparent, Virgos will strive to maintain perfect order in at least one area of their lives. It is this desire for the elimination of impurity that gives Virgo reign over the intestines in the body. The dross is sorted out while the assimilation of the valuable nutrients is allowed to take place. So, too, the Virgo is challenged to extract the positive elements in life despite the simultaneous existence of the negative.

This eerie Virgo floats at the center of *The Month of August* from the great fresco cycle in the Palazzo Schifanoia, Ferrara

VIRGO

27 THEODORE DREISER
American author

LYNDON BAINES JOHNSON
American President

28 JOHANN VON GOETHE
German author

CHARLES BOYER
French actor

29 OLIVER WENDELL HOLMES
American author; physician

INGRID BERGMAN
Swedish actress

30 MARY SHELLEY
English author

RAYMOND MASSEY
Canadian actor

31 WILLIAM SAROYAN
American author

MARIA MONTESSORI
Italian educator

1 ENGELBERT HUMPERDINCK
German composer

ROCKY MARCIANO
American boxer

2 CLEVELAND AMORY
American author

ROMARE BEARDEN
American painter

VIRGO

SEPTEMBER

3   LOUIS HENRI SULLIVAN
American architect

LOREN EISELEY
American anthropologist

4   JESSE JAMES
American outlaw

FRANÇOIS DE CHATEAUBRIAND
French author

5   ARTHUR KOESTLER
English author

JOHN CAGE
American composer

6   MARQUIS DE LAFAYETTE
French general; statesman

BILLY ROSE
American producer; composer

7   GRANDMA MOSES
American painter

QUEEN ELIZABETH I
English monarch

8   PETER SELLERS
English comedian

ANTONIN DVOŘÁK
Czech composer

9   LEO TOLSTOY
Russian author

CARDINAL RICHELIEU
French statesman

VIRGO   Portrayals of the planets and their "children," such as this one of
Mercury disputing with scholars, were popular in the Middle Ages

SEPTEMBER

10 SIR JOHN SOANE
English architect

ELSA SCHIAPARELLI
French couturière

11 O. HENRY
American author

D. H. LAWRENCE
English author

12 MAURICE CHEVALIER
French entertainer

H. L. MENCKEN
American editor; author; critic

13 SHERWOOD ANDERSON
American author

CLAUDETTE COLBERT
American actress

14 MARGARET SANGER
American social reformer

ZOË CALDWELL
Australian actress

15 JAMES FENIMORE COOPER
American author

WILLIAM HOWARD TAFT
American President; jurist

16 JEAN ARP
French sculptor

JOHN KNOWLES
American author

VIRGO One of thirty-seven movable circles from the *Astronomicum Caesareum* (1540) for solving astronomical and astrological problems

SEPTEMBER

17 FREDERICK VON STEUBEN
German soldier

ANNE BANCROFT
American actress

18 SAMUEL JOHNSON
English author

GRETA GARBO
Swedish-American actress

19 WILLIAM GOLDING
English author

ROSEMARY HARRIS
English actress

20 UPTON SINCLAIR
American author; socialist

SOPHIA LOREN
Italian actress

21 H. G. WELLS
English author

GIROLAMO SAVONAROLA
Italian religious reformer

22 PAUL MUNI
American actor

MICHAEL FARADAY
English scientist

23 AUGUSTUS CAESAR
Roman emperor

LOUISE NEVELSON
American sculptor

VIRGO   This page from the *Très Riches Heures* depicts a party of aristocratic
hawkers and peasants swimming on a hot August day

LIBRA SEPTEMBER 24 – OCTOBER 23

A major point in the year's cycle is reached at the time of the fall equinox, when the sun enters the sign of Libra and the day and night are briefly of equal length again. The first six signs of the zodiac have completed the maturation of the individual personality; now, at the equinoctial pause before the darkness prevails once again, the individual is on the threshold of participation in the larger social whole. The process of self-purification through service which Virgo has just experienced makes possible the equal partnerships symbolized by the sign of Libra, spanning the period from approximately September 24 to October 23.

Libra is the second air sign to appear in the zodiacal sequence. Air, the constantly moving molecules which flow in and around us all, provokes in its signs an awareness of these invisible threads connecting us to all others. In Gemini, this excited sense of awareness sought ever-new sources of mental stimulation; in Libra, the airy sensibility is affected by the equinoctial point of balance. As a result, Libra rules relationships on a one-to-one level, like marriages and partnerships.

The energy of Libra appropriately complements that of its polar opposite, Aries. Where Aries is driven to wage war when faced with opposition, Libra desires to compromise and cooperate. Where Aries is fiercely independent, Libra intentionally seeks out relationships. In fact, the Libra feels quite incomplete when isolated from interpersonal relationships because it is only through such dynamic interaction that this type realizes a sense of self.

For this reason, it is a challenge for Librans to maintain a sense of separateness within an ongoing relationship.

The attributes of Libra are inextricably bound up with the rulership of Venus over the sign. Venus's aesthetic influence over Taurus was responsible for the burst of green foliage in the spring; now, she paints the fall scene with splashes of intense color in a last revel before winter's sparseness. Librans often possess the particular gifts of Venus and Aphrodite: graceful charm of figure and manner, an idealization of romantic love.

The pleasing ways of Librans usually create personalities as attractive as their physical presences. Librans use this appeal to enjoy an active social life and to achieve their aims through sweetness and consideration. As a result, this sign frequently predominates in the diplomat, the person who must bring people together in a harmonious blend, or the agent who can successfully promote the talents of others.

When Aphrodite attempted to fight the Trojans and was slightly wounded on her delicate hand, Zeus comforted her with the words that she was intended only for the sweetness of love, and not for war. This might not be of comfort to the Libran who shrinks from battle in a desire to be pleasing and who is accused at times of vacillation because of efforts to maintain harmony by being all things to all people.

Among Venus's kindly influences is also the talent for artistic and musical creation. The sense of harmony that is so intrinsic to Libra draws this type to artistic endeavors, and its appreciation for finely proportioned objects reflects the symmetry of Libra's symbol, the scales. In the Libran's love for music and art, the same sensibility for melodic harmony and delicate balance prevails.

The scales evolved as Libra's symbol from the early Greek and Roman labeling of the sign as a "yoke," connoting the idea of the bond of partnership. Later, the Romans latinized the name of the sign to Libra, representing weight or measure, and thus initiated the image of the scales. This facet of the symbol introduces the idea of justice and truth, for the Libra has a strong ability to discern the point of balance in order to arrive at a fair solution. The symbolism of Libra is graphically embodied in the Egyptian myth of the goddess Maat. Maat was considered the goddess of truth, justice, and the law. When someone died, it was believed that his or her soul would first have to pass through an enormous hall where the gods would determine its fate. In the hall was a large set of scales. On one side would be placed the heart of the deceased; on the other, Maat herself would stand. If the scales achieved equilibrium, the soul would be able to pass on satisfactorily.

The glyph for the sign (♎) signifies the setting sun, as Libra marks the point when the nightly stretch of darkness will begin to outweigh the daily amount of sun; it can also be seen as a balance beam. In the natural world, Libra claims all sweet and pretty growing things, like strawberries, pansies, violets, and primroses. The parts of the body considered Libra's domain are the diaphragm and kidneys, since they fall at the waistline, as Libra falls at the equinox. In fact, Libra is not only the balance point of the entire zodiac, but quite aptly strikes equilibrium between Virgo's ascetic purity and Scorpio's devouring passions.

Libra, from a Turkish manuscript of 1582; the figure holding the scales represents Venus

LIBRA

27

THOMAS NAST
American cartoonist

GEORGE CRUIKSHANK
English caricaturist

28

MARCELLO MASTROIANNI
Italian actor

BRIGITTE BARDOT
French actress

29

MICHELANGELO ANTONIONI
Italian film director

ADMIRAL NELSON
British naval hero

30

TRUMAN CAPOTE
American author

DEBORAH KERR
British actress

1

VLADIMIR HOROWITZ
Russian-American pianist

JULIE ANDREWS
English singer; actress

2

MOHANDAS GANDHI
Indian political and
spiritual leader

GROUCHO MARX
American comedian

3

THOMAS WOLFE
American author

ERIK BRUHN
Danish ballet dancer

LIBRA

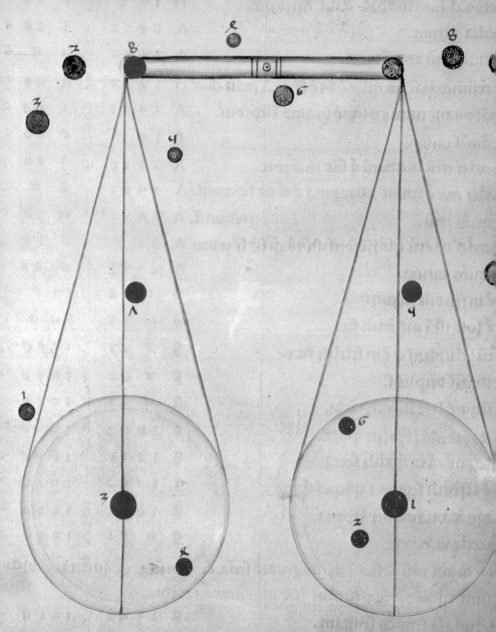

OCTOBER

4
BUSTER KEATON
American comedian

FREDERIC REMINGTON
American painter

5
DENIS DIDEROT
French encyclopedist

JONATHAN EDWARDS
American theologian

6
JENNY LIND
Swedish opera singer

LE CORBUSIER
French architect

7
R. D. LAING
British psychiatrist

RITA HAYWORTH
American actress

8
DAMON RUNYON
American author

EDDIE RICKENBACKER
American aviator

9
JOHN LENNON
English singer; songwriter

MIGUEL DE CERVANTES
Spanish author

10
GIUSEPPE VERDI
Italian composer

ANTOINE WATTEAU
French painter

LIBRA   The star catalog of al-Sufi (964) was widely circulated in 13th-century
Europe; this Libra is from the finest surviving version

11 ELEANOR ROOSEVELT
American humanitarian

GEORGE AULT
American painter

12 ROBERT COLES
American psychiatrist; author

WALLACE STEVENS
American poet

13 YVES MONTAND
French actor

LILLIE LANGTRY
English actress

14 LILLIAN GISH
American actress

HANNAH ARENDT
German-American author

15 FRIEDRICH NIETZSCHE
German philosopher

OSCAR WILDE
Irish author and wit

16 DAVID BEN-GURION
Israeli statesman

EUGENE O'NEILL
American playwright

17 ARTHUR MILLER
American playwright

MONTGOMERY CLIFT
American actor

LIBRA

Botticelli's quintessentially Libran Venus reflects his immersion
in Renaissance humanism, classical myth, and medieval astrology

OCTOBER

18 GEORGE C. SCOTT
American actor

HENRI LOUIS BERGSON
French philosopher

19 AUGUSTE LUMIÈRE
French photographic pioneer

JOHN LE CARRÉ
English author

20 BELA LUGOSI
Hungarian actor

SIR CHRISTOPHER WREN
English architect

21 SAMUEL TAYLOR COLERIDGE
English poet

ALFRED NOBEL
Swedish chemist; philanthropist

22 FRANZ LISZT
Hungarian composer; pianist

SARAH BERNHARDT
French actress

23 PIERRE LAROUSSE
French lexicographer

ROBERT BRIDGES
English poet

LIBRA
Saturn in fall in Aries, exalted in Libra (above);
Jupiter in fall in Capricorn, exalted in Cancer (below)

SCORPIO

As the nights grow longer and the air cools with the suggestion of winter's approach, the sign of Scorpio arrives. Scorpio brings the element of water, the emotional quality, to the relationship formed by Libra. The pleasant and sociable Libran has made contact on a one-to-one basis; Scorpio now deepens and consummates the bond through intense personal encounter. As the trees become bare, the realities of life and death come into sharp focus. Scorpio, occurring from approximately October 24 to November 22, oversees these transformations.

This sign has been much maligned because of its connection with the darker side of life. Coming when it does during the annual cycle, Scorpio necessarily brings up the issue of death. As its polar opposite, Taurus, reveled in May with rich greenery, Scorpio ushers in the complementary process of decay. The leaves of late autumn wither, fall on the ground, and rot; yet the nutrients that are produced in the process will be the food for next May's bounty. This factor of death for the purpose of regeneration is the critical key to Scorpio.

Instinctively, the Scorpio type has a sense of involvement with such a primal process. Knowing that long winter days lie ahead, the Scorpio is compelled to take the harmonious Libran relationship further into a total merging with the Other. The relationships of Scorpio types are thus often extremely intense, emotional, and possessive, for they must confront all those sensations lying beneath the surface in order to feel alive and to grow. For this reason, Scorpio governs the process of psychoanalysis, the peeling away of outer layers to discover the bare truth within. The defenses of the Scorpio type must necessarily die for the unbound self to emerge, and it is this process of transformation that the Scorpio is challenged to pursue.

The problems that arise from such a search into the depths are well embodied by the symbol of the scorpion, an ominous little creature which grasps its prey in its claws, then stings it to death with its poisonous tail. While satisfying their need for profound emotional confrontation, Scorpios can be capable of their namesake's devouring manipulations. The third of the signs concerned with the use of power (after Taurus and Leo), the Scorpio knows full well the potency it carries in its tail and, if provoked, will use it. Yet, the opposite extreme of passion is also possible, for Scorpio types can be staunchly devoted, committed to weathering any crisis with those few to whom they feel bonded.

The fervor of Scorpio's feelings arises from the rulership of the planet Mars over the sign (a rulership that is shared with Pluto). Mars's influence is clearly sexual when it is manifest through Scorpio. The raw, aggressive power of the red planet harnessed here to the libido produces the Scorpio's drive for the perfect sexual coupling. The metaphor frequently used by Shakespeare of the sexual act as a kind of death, with the promise of rebirth, has parallels in Scorpio's process of transformation. While Mars's influence can be seen at times in the more ruthless and vengeful type of Scorpio behavior, the drive and energy of this planet also give Scorpios persistence and the ability to go right to the heart of every matter, making them excellent investigators.

The more recently discovered planet of Pluto also reveals qualities of Scorpio—those associated with the god Pluto's under-

C'est la naente se cay mes dukler
va saluoir z cemuaillier   z adam eccant
h ler mect cay m anskes de lun

☙ Dctobre a.xxi.iours
Et lalune .xxx.
samt .xxxi.

ground activities. Pluto's influence can make the Scorpio type secretive, burying its treasure of penetrating vision in the subterranean recesses, afraid to let its powerful emotions surface. The image of the volcano elucidates this Plutonian energy, for the underlying magma of the psyche smolders and seethes until the pressure becomes overwhelming and explodes. The power of the scorpion coupled to the watery depths of feeling creates the challenge for self-knowledge and emotional self-mastery which is the ultimate Scorpio experience. Once accomplished, the Scorpio type can be an incredibly astute psychologist or physician and can bring about the transformation of others.

The scorpion appeared as an astrological symbol on Babylonian boundary stones as early as 1100 B.C. In Egypt, the goddess Selket wore the scorpion on her head as her sacred animal. The goddess of conjugal union, she was also involved in preparing the dead for embalming. From the Greeks there is the legend of Orion the Hunter who was punished for a boast that he would kill off all the animals of Crete with the poisonous sting of the scorpion. As a result, when the constellation Scorpio rises, Orion disappears below the horizon.

The glyph (♏) for Scorpio contains the image of the scorpion's barbed tail. In the natural world, Scorpio rules such plants as leeks, blackthorn, and horehound. Horehound is used in cough and cold remedies, and thus gives a clue to Scorpio's bodily regions, for the sign rules the nose and mucous membranes as well as the sexual organs. If the Scorpio can channel to a spiritual plane the considerable power held within its anatomical domain, the resulting gift of psychological profundity can be harnessed for the benefit of all.

From the *Rohan Hours,* Scorpio, symbolizing death and time, dominates a scene of peasants harvesting grapes for wine

SCORPIO

OCTOBER/NOVEMBER

27 DYLAN THOMAS
Welsh poet

THEODORE ROOSEVELT
American President

28 ERASMUS
Dutch humanist

JONAS EDWARD SALK
American microbiologist

29 JAMES BOSWELL
English diarist; biographer

FANNY BRICE
American comedienne

30 EZRA POUND
American poet

ALFRED SISLEY
French painter

31 JAN VERMEER
Dutch painter

JOHN KEATS
English poet

1 STEPHEN CRANE
American author

BENVENUTO CELLINI
Italian sculptor; author

2 DANIEL BOONE
American frontiersman

MARIE ANTOINETTE
French queen

SCORPIO

NOVEMBER

3 ANDRÉ MALRAUX
French author;
political figure

WILLIAM CULLEN BRYANT
American poet; critic

4 WILL ROGERS
American humorist

PAULINE TRIGÈRE
French-born couturière

5 ROY ROGERS
American actor

VIVIEN LEIGH
English actress

6 JOHN PHILIP SOUSA
American bandleader;
composer

MIKE NICHOLS
American director

7 MARIE CURIE
Polish-French chemist;
physicist

ALBERT CAMUS
French author

8 KATHARINE HEPBURN
American actress

MARGARET MITCHELL
American author

9 IVAN TURGENEV
Russian author

MARIE DRESSLER
American actress

SCORPIO   Mantegna's Mars, traditional ruler of Scorpio, his thigh and
cloak shaded in red, sits between Diana and a seductive Venus

NOVEMBER

10
MARTIN LUTHER
German religious reformer

RICHARD BURTON
Welsh actor

11
FEODOR DOSTOYEVSKY
Russian author

EDOUARD VUILLARD
French painter

12
AUGUSTE RODIN
French sculptor

ELIZABETH CADY STANTON
American suffragette

13
ROBERT LOUIS STEVENSON
Scottish author

EUGÈNE IONESCO
French playwright

14
CLAUDE MONET
French painter

PRINCE CHARLES
English royalty

15
GEORGIA O'KEEFFE
American painter

MARIANNE MOORE
American poet

16
GEORGE S. KAUFMAN
American playwright; critic

PAUL HINDEMITH
German composer

SCORPIO   A Persian painting of 1341 pairs the Moon in various phases (indicated
by the shading on her face) with Virgo, Libra, and Scorpio

17

AGNOLO BRONZINO
Italian painter

FIELD MARSHAL MONTGOME[
British military leader

18

ASA GRAY
American botanist

LOUIS JACQUES DAGUERRE
French photography pioneer

19

INDIRA GANDHI
Indian political leader

FERDINAND DE LESSEPS
French engineer; diplomat

20

ROBERT F. KENNEDY
American political figure

ALISTAIR COOKE
Anglo-American journalist

21

VOLTAIRE
French author; philosopher

RENÉ MAGRITTE
Belgian painter

22

GEORGE ELIOT
English author

ANDRÉ GIDE
French author

SCORPIO　　In this 16th-century Flemish tapestry, Scorpio is associated
with Jupiter, traditional ruler of Sagittarius

SAGITTARIUS

Sagittarius begins the final round of the last four signs of the zodiac. Scorpio has profoundly explored the possibilities of all-encompassing bonded relationship. As winter settles in, it is Sagittarius's time to develop a sense of integration between the individual and society as a whole. It is thus perfectly appropriate for the gregarious and expansive sign of Sagittarius to rule over the Thanksgiving/Christmas holiday season, from approximately November 23 to December 21.

Scorpio has brought awareness of death into human consciousness; Sagittarius has to deal with this grim reality as well as with the restrictions of wintertime. Strong Sagittarius types find solutions in social festivities, physical exercise, and philosophical reflection through the long cold nights. Sagittarius is the final fire sign appearing in the zodiacal sequence. The element of fire is here shaded with enlightened mental activity, for restless Sagittarians seek to evaluate their experiences in order to arrive at a framework for living, a code of ethics that can be applied to their fellow men as well as to themselves. Sagittarius instinctively feels the need for arriving at a proper philosophy of life, for understanding universal truths that will give life a meaning and purpose through the barren months ahead.

The sign of Sagittarius is symbolized by an interesting creature: the centaur who is also an archer, his upper half human and his lower half equine. A similar dichotomy is clearly seen in the two distinct representatives of this sign. The first type of Sagittarian functions more from the animal half of its symbol. The power and speed of the horse are reflected in a love of excitement, of high living and casual relationships that satisfy the need for freedom of movement and constant variety. A sheer physical need for dynamic action often finds expression in athletics or car and motorcycle racing. A restless nature coupled with a brutal physicality echoes the reputation of the centaur for uncouth and at times cruel behavior.

But the centaurs were not only crude beings; they were also known for their wisdom and scholarly expertise. The centaur Chiron, who raised many a Greek hero with the benefits of his considerable knowledge of philosophy, the arts, and medicine, was honored by Zeus by being fixed permanently in the skies as the constellation Sagittarius. This type of Sagittarian reflects the human half of the centaur, the one which is able to use the particularly human gift of faith to weather the difficulties of winter.

The human part of the centaur/archer shoots his arrows upwards, signifying the Sagittarian's belief that humanity will prevail only by realizing its singular, enlightened purpose in the cosmic scheme. Sagittarius encourages a strong sense of faith in the future, knowing that the well-directed arrow is apt to reach its mark. For this reason, types of this sign may be endowed with a special prophetic foresight, an extraordinary ability to formulate likely potentials for the future by evaluating the past. It is also why this type enjoys the prospect of a future project much more than the one at hand.

One goal that Sagittarius will always promote is a uniform code of law and ethics for all. Drawing upon an innate desire for universality, the Sagittarian type may well slight the individual in the interests of the collective. Such a type feels more comfortable with established ways of doing things, with the social and religious codes that keep Scorpio's excesses under control. In fact, Sagittarians may be accused of self-righteousness, often firmly believing that God is on their side alone. An intense example of this sort of attitude is the Spanish Inquisition, Spain being a nation under the rulership of Sagittarius.

The planetary rulership of the sign strengthens its connections with the divine, for Sagittarius is ruled by Jupiter. Jupiter, the Roman version of Zeus, embodied the idea of celestial brilliance centered in a supreme ruler. Like Zeus, Jupiter was the protector of the state, the divine educator in the ways of justice, truth, law, and morality. This mythological heritage explains Sagittarius's connections with organized religion, the encoded law, higher education, and social service organizations. In addition to these serious occupations, Zeus was infamous for his more playful, wide-ranging exploits. So, too, the Sagittarius type loves adventure, travel, and generally doing things on a grandiose scale.

The glyph for the sign (♐) symbolizes the dichotomy of half man/half horse, as well as the archer's arrow. The sign is said to rule wild plants like wood betony, agrimony, and mallows. In the body, Sagittarius has domain over the pelvic and thigh regions, which control locomotion, and over the liver, an organ known to suffer particularly from excessive living habits. The Sagittarian type is thus challenged to master the lower half of its nature, to temper its irresponsible, fast-paced life-style with the philosophical precepts which deepen the experience of life.

This Islamic Sagittarius, painted on silk, combines
precise astronomical observation with refined color and line

SAGITTARIUS

26

CHARLES SCHULZ
American cartoonist

GEORGE SEGAL
American sculptor

27

JAMES AGEE
American author

MADAME DE MAINTENON
French wife of Louis XIV

28

WILLIAM BLAKE
English poet; engraver

NATALIA MAKAROVA
Russian ballerina

29

LOUISA MAY ALCOTT
American author

JAMES ROSENQUIST
American painter

30

WINSTON CHURCHILL
English statesman

JONATHAN SWIFT
English author

1

WOODY ALLEN
American comedian; filmmaker

MARY MARTIN
American actress; singer

2

GEORGES SEURAT
French painter

MARIA CALLAS
Greek-American
opera singer

SAGITTARIUS

DECEMBER

3 NICCOLÒ AMATI
Italian violin maker

GILBERT STUART
American portrait painter

4 THOMAS CARLYLE
Scottish author; historian

EDITH LOUISA CAVELL
English nurse

5 WALT DISNEY
American film pioneer

OTTO PREMINGER
Viennese filmmaker

6 DAVE BRUBECK
American jazz pianist

JOSEPH CONRAD
English author

7 WILLA CATHER
American author

GIOVANNI LORENZO BERNINI
Italian sculptor; architect

8 JAMES THURBER
American humorist

ELI WHITNEY
American inventor

9 JOHN MILTON
English poet

HERMIONE GINGOLD
English actress

SAGITTARIUS A ceiling in the Farnesina, Rome, portrays the horoscope
of Roman banker Agostino Chigi, born December 1, 1466

DECEMBER

10
EMILY DICKINSON
American poet

RUMER GODDEN
English author

11
FIORELLO LA GUARDIA
American politician

ALEXANDER SOLZHENITSYN
Russian author

12
FRANK SINATRA
American popular singer

HELEN FRANKENTHALER
American painter

13
GUSTAVE FLAUBERT
French author

HEINRICH HEINE
German poet

14
NOSTRADAMUS
French astrologer; physician

P. PUVIS DE CHAVANNES
French painter

15
MAXWELL ANDERSON
American playwright

GEORGE ROMNEY
English portrait painter

16
LUDWIG VAN BEETHOVEN
German composer

JANE AUSTEN
English author

SAGITTARIUS This fresco depicts Jupiter, ruler of Sagittarius, as he bursts through the zodiac, hurling thunderbolts at the Titans

DECEMBER

17
ERSKINE CALDWELL
American author

ARTHUR FIEDLER
American conductor

18
PAUL KLEE
Swiss painter

BETTY GRABLE
American actress

19
JEAN GENET
French playwright

HENRY CLAY FRICK
American industrialist

20
IRENE DUNNE
American actress

PIETER DE HOOCH
Dutch painter

21
BENJAMIN DISRAELI
British statesman

HEINRICH BÖLL
German author; playwright

SAGITTARIUS Sagittarius and Capricorn appear in an Islamic manuscript
on the use of astrology in diagnosing and treating illness

ثمانية وعشرون كوكبا من الصورة وليس حوالى الصورة شئ من الكواكب
المرصودة والعرب تسمى
الاثنين اللذين على القرن
الثانى سعدا الذابح لان
احدهما نير والاخر خفى
فسمى الكبير الذابح والصغير
الملاصق له قالوا انه شاة
يذبحها ويسمى الاثنين

التى بين اللذين على الذنب الجنوب وهن صورتها كوكبة الدلو

كواكبها اثنان واربعون كوكبا من الصورة وثلث خارج الصورة والعرب تسمى على
منكبه الايمن يسمى سعد الملك واللذين على منكبه الايسر مع الذى على نب الجدى سعد السعود

CAPRICORN DECEMBER 22 – JANUARY 20

After the philosophically inclined Sagittarius, Capricorn comes prepared to implement abstract principles into solid institutional structures. While its polar opposite, Cancer, symbolized the individual within the context of the family matrix, Capricorn represents the individual within the collective context of the state. The sign marks another annual turning point, the winter solstice, and extends approximately from December 22 to January 20.

The solstice in Capricorn brings the heart of winter and the longest nights. It is a period that emphasizes the need for patience and endurance. Yet, it is also a moment that promises the rebirth of spring, for now the sun will turn and climb northward again, steadily increasing in light and warmth. Instinctively aware of this important turning point, the earthy Capricorn is willing to work hard and wait for later rewards. There is an underlying faith that self-discipline and patience will ultimately bring recognition for one's accomplishments.

Capricorn appears in the tenth place in the zodiacal circle, at the very top. A need to be at the top is typical of the Capricorn type and is suitably reflected in its symbol, the goat or sea-goat. This mythical creature has the tail of a fish and the upper body of a goat. Like the sun, which in Capricorn's time rises from the darkness of its far southern latitude, the sea-goat rises from the watery depths to claim his mountaintop position on the land. The origin of this singular beast, combining the profundity of the water element with the practical orientation of earth, is in the Babylonian god Ea. Ea, portrayed as a goat with a fish's tail, was a god of supreme wisdom. He also presided over human work: carpenters, stonecutters, and goldsmiths worshiped him. Ea suggests Capricorn because this type, although strongly bound to the workaday world of matter, is also capable of reaching the loftiest heights of spiritual renewal through a determined effort to overcome all obstacles.

It is true that Capricorns must strive consciously for contact with their "fishy" or feeling side, the submerged side that connects with the primordial source of life. Their natural affinity for earthly endeavor often deludes them into believing that achievement is everything. Capricorn types can be workaholics for whom life's only boon is the achievement of prestige for their labors. Yet, it is revealing that the sign of Capricorn should include the birthday of Christ, who was symbolized as a "fish."

Christ's role as the scapegoat for mankind's sins finds parallels in the Capricorn type's willingness to undertake enormous responsibilities that many a less hardy person would spurn. Through bearing these burdens with a persevering spirit, the Capricorn may indeed achieve wisdom in later years. Types of this sign often struggle through difficult childhoods, but eventually learn to have more control over their experiences and therefore to create less painful ones.

Being in control is essential to Capricorn and stems from the planet Saturn's rulership. Saturn was a Roman agricultural god associated with working and the riches of the earth. Every year from December 17 to December 23 (marking the winter solstice) the Romans celebrated the Saturnalia, during which the god's idol was released from the woolen strips that bound it the rest

of the year. Saturn the planet is similarly bound by its rings of ice and rock. The symbolic nature of this planet is thus one of restriction for the purpose of crystallizing experience. As a result, Capricorn types usually have an innate awareness of limitations which enables them to focus single-mindedly on a goal. From the same source, the Capricorn's strong sense of structure aids in building an ordered, functioning society, layer upon layer, as the goat scales the perilous cliffs to the top. A natural executive who takes the climb seriously, Capricorn also often displays a sense of humor and wit that help alleviate such heavy responsibilities.

The glyph for the sign (♑) symbolizes the goat's horns and head connected to the fish's tail. In the natural world, Capricorn rules plants that are connected with the color black, like black poppy and henbane, as well as those, like mossy growths and lichen, which are attached to rocks, ruled by Saturn. (Because of the structured sense of order inherent to Capricorn, this type does tend to see things in "black or white.") In the body, Capricorn rules all structural elements of anatomy: bones, teeth, skin, nails, and specifically the knees. A tendency toward psychological rigidity in this sign is reflected in its susceptibility to arthritis. The Capricorn type is thus challenged to learn to bend more with life's unpredictable turnings, for insistent clinging to structures, even ones so carefully built, can result in painful ossification.

The zodiac was a favorite motif in synagogues from the 3rd through the 6th century; this Capricorn comes from Dura Europos

CAPRICORN

DECEMBER

25
CLARA BARTON
American organizer of Red Cross

SIR ISAAC NEWTON
English mathematician;
philosopher

26
HENRY MILLER
American author

MAO TSE-TUNG
Chinese statesman

27
LOUIS PASTEUR
French chemist

MARLENE DIETRICH
German-American actress

28
WOODROW WILSON
American President

MAGGIE SMITH
English actress

29
PABLO CASALS
Spanish cellist; conductor

WILLIAM GLADSTONE
British statesman

30
RUDYARD KIPLING
English author
SIMON GUGGENHEIM
American capitalist;
philanthropist

31
HENRI MATISSE
French painter

JACQUES CARTIER
French explorer

CAPRICORN

JANUARY

1

J. D. SALINGER
American author

BETSY ROSS
American colonial patriot

2

ISAAC ASIMOV
American author; scientist

ERNST BARLACH
German sculptor

3

J. R. R. TOLKIEN
English author

CICERO
Roman orator

4

JAKOB GRIMM
German folklorist

LOUIS BRAILLE
French inventor

5

DIANE KEATON
American actress

YVES TANGUY
French painter

6

JOAN OF ARC
French saint

CARL SANDBURG
American poet; biographer

7

MILLARD FILLMORE
American President

CHARLES ADDAMS
American cartoonist

CAPRICORN In Max Ernst's *Le Capricorne*, animal parts combine to form a faintly comic couple: a fabulous goatlike king and his consort

JANUARY

8
ELVIS PRESLEY
American popular singer

LAWRENCE ALMA-TADEMA
English painter

9
SIMONE DE BEAUVOIR
French author

JOAN BAEZ
American popular singer

10
RAY BOLGER
American dancer

BARBARA HEPWORTH
English sculptor

11
WILLIAM JAMES
American philosopher

ALEXANDER HAMILTON
American statesman

12
JOHN HANCOCK
American statesman

JOHN SINGER SARGENT
American painter

13
HORATIO ALGER
American author

SOPHIE TUCKER
American popular singer

14
ALBERT SCHWEITZER
Alsatian medical missionary

BERTHE MORISOT
French painter

CAPRICORN A detail from the great rose window of Lausanne Cathedral (1275
Capricorn, Aquarius, Pisces, and the Moon surround Wate

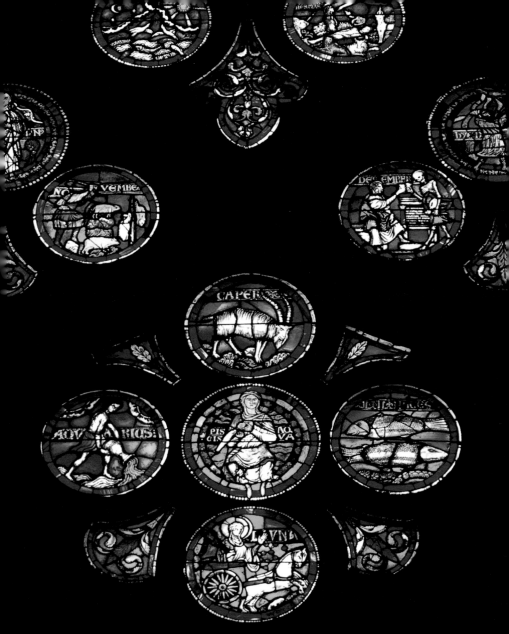

JANUARY

15
FRANCES B. JOHNSTON
American photographer

GENE KRUPA
American jazz drummer

16
ETHEL MERMAN
American popular singer

MERCE CUNNINGHAM
American choreographer

17
BENJAMIN FRANKLIN
American statesman

ANTON CHEKHOV
Russian playwright

18
A. A. MILNE
English author

MUHAMMAD ALI
American boxer

19
PAUL CÉZANNE
French painter

JANIS JOPLIN
American popular singer

20
GEORGE BURNS
American comedian

FEDERICO FELLINI
Italian film director

CAPRICORN   This 12th-century Japanese Saturn is as fierce as his Western
counterpart, although the two traditions had no common roots

北方五星眞言曰

AQUARIUS

Aquarius comes at the time of year when a restless need for stimulation stirs the blood. Winter has been too long; its monotony and isolation provoke a desire for radical change. Capricorn has dutifully confined itself to building basic societal structures proven viable over time. Now, Aquarius brings the complete fusion of the individual with the collective, this time for the purpose of introducing new ideas that will engender progress for mankind. Aquarius, the Water-bearer, energizes the time of year from approximately January 21 to February 19.

Aquarius is somewhat anomalous in its nature: it is pictured as the Water-bearer, yet its element is air. It is also the final power sign (after Taurus, Leo, and Scorpio) and one of the three signs represented by human form (Gemini and Virgo are the others). The human pictorial representation and the classification as an air sign indicate the special mental characteristics of the Aquarian type, for this sign demonstrates the power of radical ideas, of flashes of intuition that shake up the world in order to advance it.

Aquarius's airy conceptions make it a forerunner of the spring light, which is not too far away. Aquarius is the inventor, the genius (or madman), the space explorer, the revolutionary, whose unique perceptions confront Capricorn's stolid structures and demand that they change to meet present conditions. The Water-bearer is pouring forth the innovative human consciousness that will penetrate the collective awareness.

Unlike its polar opposite, Leo, the Aquarius type finds its

personal ego best expressed within the group dynamic and has an unusually strong sense of the brotherhood of man. Capricorn has developed man's relationship within a structured society; Aquarius now expands this understanding to a global level. As a result, the Aquarian type does not recognize distinctions based on nationality, social class, race, or religion, but is instead quite fascinated by the variety of mankind. Like the other air signs, Aquarians enjoy the stimulation of a wide range of contacts, but especially those with foreigners and others from markedly contrasting backgrounds.

The anomaly presented by the Aquarian type arises from the sign's simultaneous absorption within and rejection of the group. While most comfortable with a collective experience, Aquarians also feel an urgent need to be acknowledged as unique. Strongly independent, they can be provoked to unpredictable acts of rebellion if challenged by authority. This type of energy is clearly manifested in the counterculture groups that sprang up during the sixties. As a defiant gesture against the staid propriety of the preceding decade, the youth rebelled with all kinds of bizarre dress and behavior. Nevertheless, in their very search for uniqueness, they banded together in groups. This same Aquarian energy is reflected in those groups of avant-garde artists whose collective vision will not be absorbed into the mainstream until much later.

This contradictory situation is perhaps explained by the fact that Aquarius shares two rulers, the planets Saturn and Uranus. The human desire for secure foundations is sufficiently strong that the Aquarian can still be pulled back by the solidness of Capricorn, also ruled by Saturn. The Saturnine influence on the Aquarian nature contributes abilities in scientific research and invention, for the ordered process of scientific methodology works well with the type's other side, the innovative mind. Saturn also explains the loyalty of Aquarians to their more conservative friends despite their simultaneous involvement with more bohemian connections.

Uranus, on the other hand, is a great awakener and an extremely stimulating, reforming, and unpredictable kind of influence. This planet emphasizes the bright mental acuity of Aquarians which makes them so original but also conditions their impatient, eccentric, and at times thoroughly intolerant behavior toward others. Situations that hamper their individualistic freedom of action are most likely to elicit their strong-willed Uranian resistance.

The glyph for the sign (♒) symbolizes the surface of water whipped into waves by the wind. Waves are intrinsic to Aquarius, because this sign rules both air waves and electrical waves. It is the sign linked with all telecommunications, including the telepathic. Mythologically, the human symbol for Aquarius is associated with Ganymede, a handsome youth chosen by Zeus to be the cup-bearer of the gods. In the natural world, Aquarius rules frankincense and myrrh, two exotic substances which, when burned, float on the air and stimulate the senses and imagination. In the body, it holds domain over the ankles and the electrical connections in the nervous system. Like Sagittarius, Aquarius has physical rulerships that indicate a need for constant movement and excitement. The challenge for Aquarians is to be able to actualize their need for an ever-flowing network of change without overloading the circuits.

This gaunt Aquarius from a French Book of Hours evokes
the stark simplicity of medieval country life

AQUARIUS

JANUARY

24
EDITH WHARTON
American author

ROBERT MOTHERWELL
American painter

25
VIRGINIA WOOLF
English author

ROBERT BURNS
Scottish poet

26
PAUL NEWMAN
American actor

DOUGLAS MacARTHUR
American general

27
WOLFGANG AMADEUS MOZART
Austrian composer

LEWIS CARROLL
English author

28
JACKSON POLLOCK
American painter

COLETTE
French author

29
W. C. FIELDS
American comedian

THOMAS PAINE
Anglo-American political theorist

30
FRANKLIN DELANO ROOSEVELT
American President

BARBARA TUCHMAN
American historian; author

AQUARIUS

31 FRANZ SCHUBERT
Austrian composer

JACKIE ROBINSON
American baseball player

1 JOHN FORD
American film director

LANGSTON HUGHES
American poet

2 JAMES JOYCE
Irish author

JASCHA HEIFETZ
Russian-American violinist

3 GERTRUDE STEIN
American author

ELIZABETH BLACKWELL
American physician

4 CHARLES LINDBERGH
American aviator

FERNAND LÉGER
French painter

5 WILLIAM BURROUGHS
American author

SIR ROBERT PEEL
English statesman

6 CHRISTOPHER MARLOWE
English playwright

FRANÇOIS TRUFFAUT
French film director

AQUARIUS A page from a 15th-century manuscript shows Saturn, a ruler of
Aquarius, with his children: rascals, thieves, and thugs

FEBRUARY

7 CHARLES DICKENS
English author

SINCLAIR LEWIS
American author

8 EDITH EVANS
English actress

ELIZABETH BISHOP
American poet

9 GYPSY ROSE LEE
American entertainer

AMY LOWELL
American poet

10 BORIS PASTERNAK
Russian author

CHARLES LAMB
English essayist

11 THOMAS A. EDISON
American inventor

KASIMIR MALEVICH
Russian painter

12 ABRAHAM LINCOLN
American President

COTTON MATHER
American minister; author

13 GRANT WOOD
American painter

BESS TRUMAN
American First Lady

AQUARIUS In their Eastern travels, Aquarius acquired a well and Sagittarius shed his horse for a dragon growing out of his tail

جوزماه بجدی شدلکن مهمانی   کاریزک دحوی اکربتوانی
سله خر وحار بای اکرزداری   درعلم سرو

ردلوکر ترا باستد زر   اسباب
دیو کیلان ومشایخ نکوست   منعمت

FEBRUARY

14
JACK BENNY
American comedian

THOMAS R. MALTHUS
English population-study pioneer

15
JOHN BARRYMORE
American actor

SUSAN B. ANTHONY
American abolitionist; suffragette

16
HENRY ADAMS
American historian; philosopher

KATHARINE CORNELL
American actress

17
MARIAN ANDERSON
American opera singer

ALAN BATES
English actor

18
ANDRÉS SEGOVIA
Spanish guitarist

NICCOLÒ PAGANINI
Italian violinist

19
NICHOLAS COPERNICUS
Polish astronomer

MERLE OBERON
British actress

AQUARIUS The Indonesian zodiac is based on the Western one — Aquarius
and Sagittarius are recognizable here, among unfamiliar symbols

PISCES FEBRUARY 20 – MARCH 20

♓ The zodiac of twelve signs is completed with Pisces the Fish. Capricorn and Aquarius have brought the gradual lengthening of days as the sun again moves northward. Pisces marks the enigmatic pause that is both an end to winter and a hint of the beginning of spring, which Aries will thrust upon the world. The ice of winter starts to dissolve in anticipation of vernal activity; the thaw begins in the dark waters under the ice and works its way to the surface during the tenure of Pisces, from approximately February 20 to March 20.

As the last of the signs, Pisces adds the emotional element of water to the energies already born under Capricorn and Aquarius. Aquarius expanded the civilizing influence of Capricorn's pragmatism to a global vision; Pisces draws upon the feelings inherent in its watery element to incorporate the very cosmos itself. The Piscean nature experiences a sense of oneness with the universe that evokes the eternal vastness of the sea which is its home; it is an instinctive sensibility rooted in emotions as deep, mutable, and indecipherable as ocean currents. Extremely sensitive and impressionable, the Pisces type seeks to transcend the self by yielding to whatever current flows by, trusting in the destiny determined by some stronger force. It is this transcendence of the self which is both the great strength and utter weakness of the Pisces.

Like its pictorial symbol, two fish swimming in opposite directions but connected by a rope, the Pisces has an inherent duality of temperament. On the one hand, the type is buffeted by the tides of strong feelings and overwhelmed by harsh reality. Since the external world often does not provide the gentle buoyancy of water which fish are used to, Pisces may try to transcend life's roughness through escapism of one sort or another, including the oblivion of drugs or alcohol. Unlike critical Virgos, their opposite sign, Pisces may not exercise discrimination or cope well with practical details. Instead, they may be exploited by people unworthy of their sympathy, and may flounder in attending to material necessities. The empathic nature of Pisces can ensnare them into situations which drain their vitality, for Pisces often unconsciously absorb the negativity of others into themselves.

But when the fish change direction, the other manifestation of the urge for transcendence can be quite remarkable. Instead of becoming lost in delusion, the imaginative Pisces may become a spinner of illusions: a dancer, poet, painter, magician, actor, musician, photographer, one who rides the waves of fantasy while also dealing with the real world. In addition to the enormous creativity found in this sign, the Pisces type may also use its cosmic sensibility for the healing of others, as does a person like Mother Theresa, for example. Because she does not discriminate in dispensing her love, she truly exemplifies the kind of compassionate spiritual caring of which this last sign is capable. This is the side of Pisces that can be the mystic, seer, psychic, saint, or healer—an open channel for universal energies.

The heritage of the Piscean imagery is most pronounced in Christian symbolism since there are numerous references to Jesus as the "fish." Before Christianity was allowed to be practiced openly, the early Christians used the symbol of a fish (an acronym for Jesus's name) as a secret sign to reveal themselves to each other. In compassion, Jesus fed the multitudes with "five loaves and two fishes," an act designed to reveal the capacity of transcendent love to nurture. The fish has thus come to mean the submergence of the personal self to the greater whole for the purpose of the elevation of mankind, even to the extent of individual martyrdom.

The planetary ruler of Pisces is Neptune, the Roman god of the sea based on the Greek Poseidon. Carrying the trident as his symbol—now reflected in the glyph for Neptune—Poseidon was nearly as powerful as Zeus, capable of whipping up terrible storms. So, too, the Pisces type may have to undergo the ordeal of a psychological maelstrom for the purpose of ultimate cleansing. As the frozen world of winter breaks up to make way for new life, the Pisces is often forced to confront the churning, buried waters of the psyche. Despite the seeming fragility of this sign, Pisceans can reflect the strength of Poseidon in their ability to endure the most tempestuous of emotional storms.

In the natural world, Pisces rules plants that depend strongly on water for life, like seaweed, fern, and moss. In the body, Pisces rules the feet. The part of the body most constantly in touch with the ground, the feet belong to Pisces in order to help this type maintain a conscious connectedness with the solid earth, to counteract the Piscean yearning to fly away in fantasy. The glyph for the sign (♓) represents the two fish, connected by a piece of rope. When the Piscean need for experiencing union with the cosmos is tied to a sense of groundedness within the real world, the two sides of the Pisces can unite to accomplish marvelous feats which leave the spirit of all enriched.

The builders of the great Gothic cathedrals often included images of the zodiac, like this Pisces from Chartres

PISCES

FEBRUARY

23
W. E. B. DU BOIS
American sociologist; author

GEORGE FREDERICK HANDEL
German-English composer

24
WINSLOW HOMER
American painter

CHARLES LE BRUN
French painter

25
PIERRE RENOIR
French painter

GEORGE HARRISON
English popular singer

26
VICTOR HUGO
French author

BUFFALO BILL CODY
American plainsman; showman

27
H. W. LONGFELLOW
American poet

ELIZABETH TAYLOR
Anglo-American actress

28
MONTAIGNE
French essayist

STEPHEN SPENDER
English poet

29
GIOACCHINO ROSSINI
Italian composer

JIMMY DORSEY
American bandleader

PISCES

MARCH

1

DAVID NIVEN
British actor

FRÉDÉRIC CHOPIN
Polish pianist; composer

2

DR. SEUSS (THEODOR GEISEL)
American author

JENNIFER JONES
American actress

3

ALEXANDER GRAHAM BELL
American inventor

JEAN HARLOW
American actress

4

KNUTE ROCKNE
American football coach

JOHN GARFIELD
American actor

5

REX HARRISON
English actor

HOWARD PYLE
American illustrator; author

6

MICHELANGELO
Italian sculptor;
painter; architect

ELIZABETH B. BROWNING
English poet

7

MAURICE RAVEL
French composer

PIET MONDRIAN
Dutch painter

PISCES

Jupiter, ancient ruler of Pisces, holds the infant Hercules up to
Juno's breast in Tintoretto's *Origin of the Milky Way*

MARCH

8
OLIVER WENDELL HOLMES
American jurist

RUGGIERO LEONCAVALLO
Italian composer

9
AMERIGO VESPUCCI
Italian navigator

MICKEY SPILLANE
American author

10
BARRY FITZGERALD
Irish actor

FRIEDRICH VON SCHLEGEL
German poet; critic

11
TORQUATO TASSO
Italian poet

CHARLES L. EASTLAKE, JR.
English architect

12
VASLAV NIJINSKY
Russian ballet dancer

EDWARD ALBEE
American playwright

13
JOSEPH PRIESTLEY
English physician

JANET FLANNER (GENÊT)
American journalist

14
ALBERT EINSTEIN
German-American physicist

MICHAEL CAINE
English actor

PISCES

An unusual Pisces from Persia finds the two fish forming a
closed circle, head to head. The figure above is Aquarius

ماه چون درجوت اید نیک نبود ای بگفت

لیک دعوت نیک باشد دیدن اسر

هم کلاه و هم قبا و هم کمر هم سپر سن

قصد کردن دست را و پا را ن خن رفت

و اندرو نیکو بود پوشیدن این جا رنر

والجه درش باشد ابذا اجله خشیدن من

MARCH

15   ANDREW JACKSON
American President

LADY AUGUSTA GREGORY
Irish playwright

16   JAMES MADISON
American President

BARON ANTOINE GROS
French painter

17   NAT "KING" COLE
American popular singer

RUDOLF NUREYEV
Russian ballet dancer

18   STÉPHANE MALLARMÉ
French poet

NIKOLAI RIMSKY-KORSAKOV
Russian composer

19   DAVID LIVINGSTONE
Scottish explorer; missionary

SERGEI DIAGHILEV
Russian ballet impresario

20   HENRIK IBSEN
Norwegian playwright

B. F. SKINNER
American psychologist

PISCES   The painter of this Pisces continues an Islamic tradition of
astronomical accuracy largely foreign to Western conventions

LIST OF ILLUSTRATIONS

The author and publisher wish to thank the individuals and institutions who have permitted the reproduction of works in their collections. Unless otherwise stated, the owner has supplied the photograph appearing herein. The majority of the illustrations show details of larger works.

COVER

The twelve signs from the calendar of a Book of Hours. Italian (Lombardy?), c. 1475. Vellum. The Pierpont Morgan Library, William S. Glazier Collection (G. 14)

FRONTISPIECE

The Limbourg Brothers. "Zodiacal Man," from the *Très Riches Heures du Duc de Berry*. French, 1413-16. Vellum. Musée Condé, Chantilly (Photo: Draeger)

INTRODUCTION

Frontispiece to the calendar from the *Psalter of Blanche of Castille*. French, c. 1200. Vellum. Bibliothèque de l'Arsénal, Paris

"The Plan of the Universe," from a manuscript of the *Liber de proprietatibus* of Bartholomaeus Anglicus. French, 15th century. Vellum. Bibliothèque Nationale, Paris

Minai'i Ware Bowl. Iranian, late 12th-early 13th century. Glazed earthenware, polychrome, and gilt decoration. The Metropolitan Museum of Art, Rogers Fund and Gift of The Schiff Foundation, 1957

"The Triumph of Time Over Fame," from a manuscript of Petrarch's *Triumphs*. French, c. 1500. Vellum. Bibliothèque Nationale, Paris

Page from a manuscript of *Astrology and the Sun*. Thai, 19th century. Watercolor on paper. Spencer Collection. The New York Public Library. Astor, Lenox and Tilden Foundations (Photo: Philip Pocock, New York)

Table Clock. Austrian, 1545. Painted iron and bronze. Kunsthistorisches Museum, Vienna (Photo: Photo Mayer, Vienna)

Bartolommeo Passarotti. *The Astrologer*. Italian, 16th century. Oil on canvas. Galleria Spada, Rome (Photo: Ludovico Canali, Rome)

ARIES

"Aries," from *The Jamnapattra of Prince Navanibal Singh* (Sanskrit manuscript). Indian (Lahore), 19th century. Colors on paper. British Library, London (Photo: Hamlyn Group Picture Library)

"Aries," from an English manuscript, c. 1025. Vellum. British Library, London

Page from a manuscript of Thomas Norton's *Ordinall of Alchymy*. English, 15th century. Vellum. British Library, London

Attributed to Francesco Pesellino. "Mars on a Chariot of Fire," from a manuscript of Silius Staticus's *Punica*. Italian, second half of the 15th century. Detached illumination applied to panel. Biblioteca Marciana, Venice (Photo: Ludovico Canali, Rome)

TAURUS

"Taurus," from a Southern Italian astrological manuscript, c. 1220-40. Vellum. Bibliothèque Nationale, Paris

"Venus," from *Kuyō Hiraku (The Secrets of the Nine Luminaries: An Astrological Treatise)*. Japanese, early 12th century. Ink and pale colors on paper. Spencer Collection. New York Public Library. Astor, Lenox and Tilden Foundations (Photo: Philip Pocock, New York)

Francesco del Cossa and others. *The Month of April*. Italian, c. 1469. Fresco. Palazzo Schifanoia, Sala dei Mesi, Ferrara (Photo: Rizzoli, Milan)

Attributed to the Maison des Filles de la Providence, Paris. *Spring*. French, c. 1683-84. Needlepoint hanging; wool, silk, and metal threads on canvas. The Metropolitan Museum of Art, New York. Rogers Fund, 1946

GEMINI

Palintangatan, astrological calendar. Indonesian, late 19th century. Watercolor and ink on sized cotton. Spencer Collection. New York Public Library. Astor, Lenox and Tilden Foundations (Photo: Philip Pocock, New York)

Fernando Gallego. *Mercury,* from the frescos in the library vault of the University of Salamanca. Spanish, 1493-1506 (Photo: MAS, Barcelona)

Victor Brauner. *Gemini.* Romanian, 1938. Oil on canvas. Private collection

Antoine Watteau. *Ceres (Allegory of Summer).* French, c. 1712. Oil on canvas. National Gallery of Art, Washington, D.C. Samuel H. Kress Collection

CANCER

"The Moon and Venus in Cancer," from a manuscript of an astrological treatise by Albumasar. Arabic, c. 1250. Paper. Bibliothèque Nationale, Paris

"June," from *Les Heures de la Duchesse de Bourgogne.* French, c. 1450. Vellum. Musée Condé, Chantilly (Photo: Giraudon)

Plate with Sign of Cancer. German (Ludwigsburg), 1770-75. Pauls Collection, Basel (Photo: Hans Hinz, Basel)

Stained-glass Quatrefoil Panel. Austrian, c. 1380. The Metropolitan Museum of Art, Gothic Fund, 1936

LEO

Sol in Leo. Indian (Delhi?), 17th-18th century. Miniature on paper. The Pierpont Morgan Library, New York (M. 787)

The Limbourg Brothers. "July," from the *Bèlles Heures du Duc de Berry.* French, c. 1406-9. Vellum. The Metropolitan Museum of Art, The Cloisters Collection, Purchase, 1954 (Photo: Charles Passela, New York)

Gerhardt Emmoser. Astronomical Globe. Austrian, 1579. Silver, partly gilt. The Metropolitan Museum of Art, Gift of J. Pierpont Morgan, 1917

Antonio Cicognara. *The Sun.* Tarot card from a deck made for Cardinal Sforza. Italian (Cremona), 1484. Illumination on cardboard. The Pierpont Morgan Library, New York (M. 630, f. 13)

VIRGO

Francesco del Cossa and others. *The Month of August.* Italian, c. 1469. Fresco. Palazzo Schifanoia, Sala dei Mesi, Ferrara (Photo: Rizzoli, Milan)

"Mercury Disputing with Scholars," from a manuscript of Christine de Pisan's romance *L'Épître d'Othéa à Hector.* French, c. 1410-15. Vellum. British Library, London

Michaël Ostendorfer. "Volvelle," from Petrus Apianus's *Astronomicum Caesareum.* German (Ingolstadt), 1540. Woodcut. The Library of Congress, Washington, D.C.

The Limbourg Brothers. "August," from the *Très Riches Heures du Duc de Berry.* French, 1413-16. Vellum. Musée Condé, Chantilly (Photo: Bibliothèque Nationale, Paris)

LIBRA

"Libra," from *The Ascension of Propitious Stars and the Sources of Sovereignty* of Matali 'al-Sa'ada wa-manabi 'al-siyada. Turkish, 1582. Polished paper. The Pierpont Morgan Library, New York (M. 788, f. 19v)

"Libra," from *The Book of Stars and Constellations* of 'Abd al-Rahman al-Sufi. French, 13th century. Vellum. Bibliothèque de l'Arsénal, Paris

Sandro Botticelli. *The Birth of Venus.* Italian, after 1482. Paint on canvas. Uffizi, Florence (Photo: Ludovico Canali, Rome)

"Planets and Signs in Conjunction," from *The Ascension of Propitious Stars and the Sources of Sovereignty* of Matali 'al-Sa 'ada wa-manabi 'al-siyada. Turkish, 1582. Polished paper. The Pierpont Morgan Library, New York (M. 788, f. 32v-33)

SCORPIO

The Rohan Master. "October," from *Les Grandes Heures du Duc de Rohan.* French, c. 1418. Vellum. Bibliothèque Nationale, Paris

Andrea Mantegna. *Diana, Mars, and Venus.* Italian, late 15th century. Pen, brown ink, and wash, with touches of white and color. British Museum, London

"Virgo, Libra, and Scorpio." manuscript leaf from the *Munis al-Abrar* (anthology of Persian poetry) of Muhammad ibn al-Jarjarmi. Iranian, Mongol School, 1341. Colors and gilt on paper. The Metropolitan Museum of Art, The Cora Timken Burnett collection of Persian miniatures and other Persian art objects. Bequest of Cora Timken Burnett, 1957

October, tapestry, perhaps after design of Bernart van Orley. Flemish, 1525. Wool and silk. The Metropolitan Museum of Art, Bequest of Mrs. August D. Juilliard, 1916

SAGITTARIUS

"Sagittarius," from *The Book of Stars and Constellations* of 'Abd al-Rahman al-Sufi. Persian, 1632. Colors and ink on silk. Spencer Collection. The New York Public Library. Astor, Lenox and Tilden Foundations (Photo: Philip Pocock, New York)

Baldassare Peruzzi. *Sala di Galatea,* ceiling fresco. Italian, 1509-11. Farnesina, Rome (Photo: Ludovico Canali, Rome)

Perino del Vaga. *Jupiter Destroys the Titans,* ceiling fresco. Italian, c. 1530. Palazzo Doria Pamphili, Genoa (Photo: Società Arti Grafiche Editoriale, Genoa)

"Sagittarius and Capricorn," from the *Ajaib al-Makhlukat (Marvels of Creation)* of al-Kazvini. Iraqi, c. 1370-80. Freer Gallery of Art, Washington, D.C.

CAPRICORN

"Capricorn," ceiling tile from the synagogue at Dura Europos in western Syria. 3rd century A.D. The Louvre, Paris

Max Ernst. *Le Capricorne.* German, 1964. Bronze. Musée National d'Art Moderne, Paris

Stained-glass Rose Window, Cathedral of Lausanne. French, 13th century. (Photo: Painton Cowen, London)

"Saturn," from *Kuyō Hiraku (The Secrets of the Nine Luminaries: An Astrological Treatise).* Japanese, early 12th century. Ink and pale colors on paper. Spencer Collection. The New York Public Library. Astor, Lenox and Tilden Foundations (Photo: Philip Pocock, New York)

AQUARIUS

"Aquarius," from a Book of Hours. French (Normandy), c. 1440-50. Vellum. Bodleian Library, Oxford (Ms. Auct. D. inf. 2.11, fol. 1r)

"Saturnus," from a *De Sphaera* manuscript. Northern Italian, 15th century. Vellum. Biblioteca Estense, Modena (Photo: Studio Fotografico Roncaglia, Modena)

"Sagittarius, Capricorn, and Aquarius," manuscript leaf from the *Munis al-Abrar* (anthology of Persian poetry) of Muhammad ibn al-Jarjarmi. Iranian, Mongol School, 1341. Colors and gilt on paper. The Metropolitan Museum of Art, The Cora Timken Burnett collection of Persian miniatures and other Persian art objects, Bequest of Cora Timken Burnett, 1957

Palintangatan, astrological calendar. Indonesian, late 19th century. Watercolor and ink on sized cotton. Spencer Collection. New York Public Library. Astor, Lenox and Tilden Foundations (Photo: Philip Pocock, New York)

PISCES

"Pisces," stained-glass window, Cathedral of Chartres. French, 13th century (Photo: Giraudon, Paris)

Jacopo Tintoretto. *The Origin of the Milky Way.* Italian, c. 1580. Oil on canvas. The National Gallery, London

"Aquarius and Pisces," from a Persian anthology. Shiraz, 1441. Topkapi Saray Library, Istanbul (Photo: Haluk Doganbey, Istanbul)

"Pisces," from *The Book of Stars and Constellations* of 'Abd al-Rahman al-Sufi. Persian, 1632. Colors and ink on silk. Spencer Collection. New York Public Library. Astor, Lenox and Tilden Foundations (Photo: Philip Pocock, New York)

ZODIAC MEDALLIONS IN CALENDAR

Adapted from *The Astrologer of the Nineteenth Century* (London, 1825)